PICTURING
THE
BOMB

PHOTOGRAPHS
FROM THE
SECRET WORLD
OF THE
MANHATTAN
PROJECT

PICTURING

THE BOMB

PHOTOGRAPHS FROM THE SECRET WORLD OF THE MANHATTAN PROJECT

Editor: Adele Westbrook
Designer: Lorraine Ferguson

Library of Congress Cataloging-in-Publication Data

Fermi, Rachel
    Picturing the bomb : photographs from the secret world of the
Manhattan Project / introduction by Richard Rhodes; text by
Rachel Fermi and Esther Samra.
        p. cm.
    Includes biographical references and index.
    ISBN 0-8109-3735-2
    1. Nuclear bomb—United States—History. 2. Nuclear bomb—
United States—History—Pictorial works. 3. Manhattan Project
(U.S.)—History. 4. Manhattan Project (U.S.)—History—
Pictorial works.
I. Rhodes, Richard. II. Samra, Esther. III. Title.
QC773.A1F47 1995
355.8'25119'0973—dc20   94-42666

Note to the Reader
Throughout this book, the following abbreviations and references
have been used:
DOE: Department of Energy
LANL: Los Alamos National Laboratory
MED: the Manhattan Engineering District
    (also known as the Manhattan Project)
NARA: National Archives and Records Administration
    (the photographs included in this book from NARA all originate
    from the series 434-OR)
SED: Special Engineer Detachment
WAC: Women's Army Corps

Hanford refers to the Hanford Engineering Works, including
    the Hanford construction camp and the town of Richland,
    in Washington State.
Los Alamos refers to the Los Alamos laboratory in Los Alamos,
    New Mexico.
The Met Lab refers to the Metallurgical Laboratory at the
    University of Chicago, in Chicago, Illinois.
Oak Ridge refers to the Clinton Engineering Works in Oak Ridge,
    Tennessee.
Project Alberta (Project A) refers to the combat use of the atomic
    bombs, based in Wendover, Utah, and on the island of Tinian
    in the Pacific.
Trinity refers to the test and site of the first atomic bomb near
    Alamogordo, New Mexico.

CONTENTS

Page from photo album.

Los Alamos, February 1944.

Photographer: Jean Critchfield.
Courtesy of Jean Critchfield

Second House on Gold St.
Neighbors   Gene & Rudy Peoples
Helen & Rod Gordon
Laura & David Tornie

Learning To Walk

Page from photo album.

Hiroshima and Nagasaki,

September–October 1945.

"BUT, ABOVE ALL, THERE WERE THE MORAL QUESTIONS.

I KNEW SCIENTISTS HAD HOPED THAT THE BOMB

WOULD NOT BE POSSIBLE, BUT THERE IT WAS AND IT

HAD ALREADY KILLED AND DESTROYED SO MUCH.

WAS WAR OR WAS SCIENCE TO BE BLAMED?

SHOULD THE SCIENTISTS HAVE STOPPED THE WORK

ONCE THEY REALIZED THAT A BOMB WAS FEASIBLE?

WOULD THERE ALWAYS BE WAR IN THE FUTURE?

TO THESE KINDS OF QUESTIONS THERE IS NO SIMPLE

ANSWER." — Laura Fermi, in *Reminiscences of Los Alamos,* edited by Lawrence Badash

FOREWORD

BY RACHEL FERMI

MY GRANDMOTHER ASKED these questions twenty-five years after the first atomic bombs were used. This book has grown out of the complexities underlying her questions, and from my own need to understand more fully the grandfather I never knew: a physicist whose work radically altered the world he was born into and helped create the world in which I now live.

Picturing the Bomb explores these questions through photography. Photography has the capacity to give us a taste of lived experience. This is an assemblage of the private and personal, the secret and official photographs that were found in family albums and discovered in laboratory archives. Only the photographs made by those people who lived and worked inside the Manhattan Project's secret world, which ended with the bombings of Hiroshima and Nagasaki, have been included. The Manhattan Project, its principal players, and its legacy, have all been written about in great depth previously, but the extensive photographic record has been ignored. Through the sequencing and juxtaposition of images on these pages, we have tried to convey an open-ended interpretation. The images show that which was observed, recorded, and sometimes stage-managed by scientists, soldiers, and factory workers. Fifty years later, looking at the many different kinds of photographs from the Manhattan Project they form a strange and unique cultural album.

INTRODUCTION

BY RICHARD RHODES

THE FIRST ATOMIC BOMBS were handmade. American and European émigré scientists and technicians conceived, designed, and assembled them on a remote New Mexican mesa hidden in a wilderness of national forest, crated them and sent them off by truck to be shipped across the Pacific to end the Second World War. They were made of ordinary materials including common blotter paper, cork, aluminum, plastic, a touch of gold and silver, a tangle of wires and detonators, blocks of high explosives and steel armor plate, but their active hearts were shaped from exotic metals that had never before on earth been purified in quantity. These, the small rings or hemispheres of uranium or plutonium that made them uniquely destructive, had been produced in vast automated factories and remote-controlled chemical plants built in great haste in rural Tennessee and Washington State, away from prying eyes. Between 1938, when nuclear fission was discovered, and 1945, when the first atomic bombs left the mesa of Los Alamos headed for Japan, the atomic industry in the United States grew from a laboratory benchtop to an industry that matched the 1945 U.S. automobile industry in numbers of workers and physical plant. That dramatic change of scale — from two chemists in a laboratory to thousands of people laboring secretly at construction and manufacture in factories so large that supervisors patrolled them on bicycles — measures the importance American leaders attached to acquiring atomic weapons first.

They did so because the two chemists who discovered nuclear fission just before Christmas in 1938 were Germans and the laboratory was located in Berlin, the capital of Nazi Germany. Nine months after Otto Hahn and Fritz Strassmann discovered the mechanism for releasing nuclear energy in quantity, the armies of Adolf Hitler invaded Poland and began a blitz across Europe that stopped only at the Atlantic coast. The vision of Hitler's promised Thousand-Year Reich made secure with German atomic bombs horrified the British; in time they communicated their urgency to the United States.

"The deep things in science are not found because they are useful," the American theoretical physicist J. Robert Oppenheimer once observed; "they are found because it was possible to find them." Hahn and Strassmann were trying to puzzle out a mystery, as scientists do, not to invent atomic bombs. They were bombarding elements with neutrons to make transmutations which they then used their skills at radiochemistry to identify, learning more in the process about how atoms are organized. The substance that particularly interested the two German scientists in the winter of 1938 was uranium, the heaviest element known to occur on earth, ninety-second and last on the periodic table, a dense, purple-black metal that had modest commercial value as a coloring agent for pottery glazes. (In Rome in 1932, shortly after the discovery of the neutron, Enrico Fermi, a man in the top four on anyone's list of the greatest physicists of the twentieth century, had led a team that systematically worked its way up the periodic table bombarding the elements with neutrons and recording the resulting transmutations; uranium was the last piece of that larger puzzle.)

At a crucial point in their work, Hahn and Strassmann realized that neutron bombardment had somehow produced trace quantities of barium in their beaker of uranium nitrate. They were startled. A neutron might chip a few protons off a uranium nucleus and transmute it to thorium, element 90, or even actinium, element 89, but barium, element 56, was nearly half the periodic table away. They knew of no physical process that could split an atom completely in half. The two chemists reported their strange findings to their physicist colleague, Lisa Meitner, the absent third member of their team, an Austrian Jew who had recently fled Nazi Germany for Sweden. Meitner conferred over Christmas with her young physicist nephew, Otto Robert Frisch. Aunt and nephew, vacationing in a small village in western Sweden, walked in the snowy woods and thought the strange new reaction through. They visualized the uranium nucleus as a waterdrop, barely holding together against the mutual repulsion of its 92 positively-charged protons. An incoming neutron would disrupt such an unstable arrangement as violently as if the moon had struck the earth. The uranium nucleus would wobble like a water-filled balloon. On one of its wobbles, elongating like pulled taffy, a neck might form between two bulges. Then the force that held the nuclei together would reassert itself within each bulge, the neck would thin and snap and the two new, smaller nuclei, which might be almost anything but would usually be barium (56) and krypton (36) (36 + 56 = 92), each positively charged, would repel each other with enormous energy — enough energy per atom, Frisch calculated later, to make a visible grain of sand visibly jump. Back in Copenhagen, where he worked with the distinguished Danish physicist Niels Bohr, Frisch confirmed the new reaction with a physical experiment and named it with a term borrowed from biology, from the process of cell division that it resembled.

The world was still nominally at peace; no one proposed keeping the new discovery a secret. Ideas proliferate like viruses. Hahn and Strassmann, Meitner and Frisch published reports in German and British journals; Bohr carried the news to America; a French physicist wrote to his colleagues in Leningrad; a Japanese military officer who was an electrical engineer noticed the foreign journal reports. The world of physicists, still a small and collegial world, soon understood that here at last, after forty years of basic research into the mysteries of radioactivity, was a process that might release the enormous energies latent in matter that Albert Einstein had quantified in his famous formula $E = mc^2$.

It required one more round of experiments to confirm that probability. If a neutron only fissioned one uranium atom, then any large-scale release would depend upon large-scale production of neutrons, and neutrons were hard to come by. But there was reason to suspect that the two departing fragments of the former uranium atom would readjust their internal structure along the way to stabilize themselves, and in the process might eject two or more secondary neutrons. With the right arrangement of materials, two secondary neutrons might be coaxed to fission two more uranium

Enrico Fermi and Niels Bohr at the Carnegie Institution. Washington, D.C., January 1939.
Photographer: Unknown. Courtesy of Nella Fermi Weiner

atoms, which would then release four additional secondary neutrons, which would then fission four additional uranium atoms, which would then release eight secondary neutrons, fissioning eight atoms, releasing sixteen neutrons, fissioning sixteen atoms, releasing thirty-two neutrons — and so on, the process spreading through a mass of uranium exponentially until the material blew itself apart. Borrowing a term from chemistry, physicists called this process a chain reaction. In eighty-some generations of the chain, they calculated, a kilogram of uranium (an amount smaller than a golf ball) might explode with energy equivalent to twenty thousand tons of TNT. Fermi — in New York now in exile from fascist Italy — and other physicists in New York and Paris soon organized the necessary measurements. They found more than two secondary neutrons per fission. War was closer by then, in March and April 1939; one of Fermi's colleagues suggested they keep the secondary neutrons a secret, but the French refused and published their results. The world learned that an atomic bomb was possible. Within a week, physicists everywhere were sketching crude bombs on office blackboards.

Because they understood the energetics of nuclear fission — the enormous output of energy for such a small input of material — the physicists also understood almost immediately that this unexpected discovery would have major political consequences. One atomic bomb, probably not much bigger than an ordinary aerial bomb, certainly no bigger than a truck, could destroy a city. And there was no question of any atomic "secret"; the laws of physics worked as well in Berlin and Moscow as in Washington. If one country could make atomic bombs, so, sooner or later, could any other country that could afford them. "The most effective reply [to an atomic threat]," Otto Frisch and a colleague wrote the British government early in 1940, "would be a counter-threat with a similar bomb." If two countries accumulated a stock of these small, portable, holocaustal weapons, against which the only defense was a counter-threat, would either country dare to start a war?

Fortunately, building atomic bombs turned out to be more complicated than simply refining uranium. Evidently there was a certain minimum amount of uranium necessary to sustain a chain reaction, or there would be no uranium left on earth. Physicists named that minimum amount a "critical mass." "Quantities of the material less than the critical amount are quite stable," the British government concluded in 1941. ". . . On the other hand, if the amount of material exceeds the critical value it is unstable and a reaction will develop and multiply itself with enormous rapidity, resulting in an explosion of unprecedented violence." It required several years' work to determine how much uranium made a critical mass; it turned out to be more than 10 kilograms.

Nor was natural uranium explosive. Natural uranium consisted of two variant physical forms called isotopes, one part uranium 235, 139 parts uranium 238. The U238, it seemed, soaked up neutrons rather than fissioning. Only the U235 was suitable for bomb-making. But U238 and U235 were chemically identical. They could only be separated by physical means, and their only useful physical distinction was their small difference in mass: U238 was slightly heavier than U235. Natural uranium could be converted to a gas and pumped against a porous barrier, in which case the lighter U235 would diffuse through the barrier slightly faster than the U238. Or natural uranium could be vaporized in a vacuum and pulled through a curved magnetic field, in which case the lighter U235 would follow a tighter curve than the heavier U238 and the two slightly separated vapor streams could be caught in separate buckets at the apparatus's far end. But however ingenious the process, each stage of separation would be slight. Gaseous diffusion would require some 5,000 stages to enrich natural uranium up to 93 percent U235, bomb grade; the two wings of the resulting factory, an installation comparable to a major oil refinery, would each be half a mile long.

Then another possibility suggested itself. When the U238 in natural uranium encountered a neutron, it usually absorbed that neutron, which transmuted it one step farther along the periodic table into a new, manmade element which its American discoverer named neptunium, element 93. Neptunium in turn was radioactive and unstable; within a few days it changed form again. At the Radiation Laboratory in Berkeley, early in 1941, radiochemist Glenn Seaborg and his colleagues bombarded uranium with neutrons in the big Berkeley cyclotron to make neptunium, allowed the neptunium to transmute, then worked out a way to separate a few millionths of a gram of the transmutation product from its parent materials. The unknown substance had a characteristic radioactivity; it could be separated chemically from all known elements; it must be a new element, atomic number 94. In 1942, Seaborg gave it a name: plutonium. It fissioned as U235 fissioned but even more actively, producing not an average two secondary neutrons per fission but closer to four. Under suitable circumstances, six kilograms or less of plutonium would make a critical mass. Best of all from the point of view of the bomb makers, it could be separated chemically from uranium.

With encouragement from the British, who felt the Nazi breath hot on their necks, the United States government got into the atomic-bomb business on December 6, 1941, the day before the Japanese attacked the American fleet anchored in Hawaii at Pearl Harbor. Besides locating factory sites and supplies of uranium ore, one of the first challenges the secret program faced was demonstrating a chain reaction. Because a full critical mass had to be assembled to start a chain reaction, the phenomenon could not be demonstrated at laboratory scale. But Enrico Fermi and his gadfly Hungarian colleague Leo Szilard, working first at Columbia University and then moving to the University of Chicago, had devised a way to demonstrate a chain reaction in a massive, diluted form.

The secondary neutrons that came from fission were fast neutrons. An atomic bomb, to chain-react through enough generations to make a large explosion before it blew itself apart, would use those fast secondary neutrons. Any neutron, however, fast or slow, would fission U235. U238, on the other hand, absorbed fast neutrons but was impervious to slow neutrons. Fermi and Szilard realized that if they could mix natural uranium with some suitable moderating material that slowed down the secondary neutrons from fission — sneaking them under the U238 threshold, as it were — they should be able to start a chain reaction based on slow neutrons rather than fast. If they introduced a sliding rod of neutron-absorbing material into the mixture, like a throttle on an engine, they ought to be able to start, stop, and sustain the chain reaction under control.

The way to slow neutrons was to bounce them like billiard balls against atoms of similar size, forcing them to give up energy pushing the atoms around. The light elements — the hydrogen in water, the carbon in graphite — were similar in size to neutrons. After calculation and experimental measurement, Fermi and Szilard settled on graphite, the crystalline form of carbon used in pencil lead, for a neutron moderator. They would plug pieces of uranium into blocks of graphite and stack the blocks to make a rough sphere. They estimated that such an assembly would go critical when they had stacked about 45 tons of uranium with 350 tons of graphite, a system as big as a two-car garage. If it worked it would make plenty of neutrons for transmuting plutonium as well.

This slow monster of graphite and uranium Fermi christened a "pile." It could never explode like an atomic bomb, but it could explode like dynamite, spewing radioactivity. Confident that he could control it from its first hour of operation, Fermi proposed building it secretly in an underground doubles squash court under the stands of the university football stadium in the middle of the city of Chicago. The United States was at war, work toward a weapon that might end the war was measured day by day in men's lives, and the pile went up on the squash court. It was the world's first man-made nuclear reactor. Physicist Herbert Anderson, an eyewitness, describes the historic experiment on December 2, 1942, that brought it to life:

> *At first you could hear the sound of the neutron counter, clickety-clack, clickety-clack. Then the clicks came more and more rapidly, and after a while they began to merge into a roar. . . . That was the moment to switch to the chart recorder. . . . Everyone watched in the sudden silence the mounting deflection of the recorder's pen. . . . Again and again, the scale of the recorder had to be changed to accommodate the neutron intensity which was increasing more and more rapidly. Suddenly Fermi raised his hand. "The pile has gone critical," he announced.*

So the chain reaction of uranium was an accomplished fact. Fermi ran the pile for four and a half minutes and shut it down. Eugene Wigner, another Hungarian émigré on hand that day, produced a celebratory *fiasca* of Chianti. They drank from paper cups and signed the *fiasca's* straw wrapping. Leo Szilard, who had helped coax nuclear energy from its lair, was never an optimist. "There was a crowd there and then Fermi and I stayed there alone. I shook hands with Fermi and I said I thought this day would go down as a black day in the history of mankind."

While Fermi was building the pile, Eugene Wigner applied its principles to the design of large, water-cooled production reactors that would transmute U238 into plutonium in quantities sufficient to make bombs. By now the U. S. Army Corps of Engineers, in the person of Lieutenant General Leslie R. Groves, the man who had built the Pentagon, a big, hard-driving engineer, had taken over the bomb project and code-named it the Manhattan Engineer District. Groves had bought whole valleys around Oak Ridge, Tennessee, for the factories that would enrich uranium and a big desert bend along the Columbia River near Hanford, Washington, for the graphite production piles. Glenn Seaborg, now based in Chicago, was developing the separation chemistry necessary to extract plutonium from its matrix of uranium and fission byproducts after irradiation. Seaborg's process, perfected in the laboratory at microscopic scale, would be enlarged a million-fold into remote-controlled machinery operating behind thick concrete radiation shielding in windowless buildings so vast — 800 feet long and eight stories high — that construction workers nicknamed them "Queen Marys" after the British ocean liner they matched in scale. Forty-five thousand construction workers came to Hanford, lured by the promise of good wages and meat on the menu despite wartime rationing. "The most essential thing to bring with you is a padlock," a recruiting brochure announced. Du Pont, the company that would operate the installation, built saloons with windows hinged for easy tear-gas lobbing.

There was more civility in Tennessee, though tens of thousands of men and women eventually worked to build and run the uranium enrichment plants Groves decreed there. They'd been broke and bored for ten years, sitting out the Great Depression, a Tennessee man remembered long after the war, and suddenly there were jobs, excitement, a war to win, something to do. Skidmore, Owings and Merrill built a model city of prefabricated houses, the architecture firm's first large commission. Tennis courts by day became outdoor dance floors by night where romances flourished. An anonymous poet memorialized the perpetual mud of perpetual construction:

In order not to check in late,
I've had to lose a lot of weight,
From swimming through a fair-sized flood
And wading through the goddam mud.

I've lost my rubbers and my shoes
Perpetually I have the blues
My spirits tumble with a thud
Because of all the goddam mud.

It's in my system so that when
I cut my finger now and then
Instead of bleeding just plain blood
Out pours a stream of goddam mud.

Mud.
Oak Ridge, 1944.
Photographer: E. Westcott.
Courtesy of NARA

Everybody wondered what it was they were processing. On this top-secret project, Groves's policy of "compartmentalization" required that people be told only what they needed to know to do their job. Operators at elaborate work stations who adjusted the intensity of the magnetic field on the electromagnetic isotope separators were instructed only to keep the needles on their gauges within certain limits. (Tennessee country women quickly learned to control the skittish machines more efficiently than the Berkeley physicists who designed them.) Tons of waxy white solidified uranium hexafluoride came in at one end of the complexes; nothing seemed to go out the other because the production of uranium enriched to weapons' grade was measured in grams per day. An Army courier in civilian disguise picked up the output every few days in an ordinary briefcase and delivered it by train to another courier in Chicago

whose destination he didn't know; the second courier carried it on to Santa Fe for delivery to the secret laboratory on the mesa thirty miles northwest. Plutonium in nitrate solution jitneyed down from Hanford to Los Alamos in modified Army ambulances over the rough two-lane highways of the day.

The bomb laboratory had been an afterthought. Physicist Arthur Compton, who directed the operation in Chicago, had originally been assigned bomb design. He delegated the work to Oppenheimer, a wealthy New Yorker who had trained at Harvard and in Europe. Oppenheimer, rail-thin and intense, a professor at Berkeley, got the assignment because bomb design would have to be theoretical and he was the best theoretician available. In the summer of 1942 he convened a conference at Berkeley to review bomb theory. Hungarian émigré Edward Teller attended, as did German émigré Hans Bethe, American theoretician Robert Serber and half a dozen others, a first-class team.

Teller arrived with a radical new idea in his pocket which Fermi had broached almost casually — "out of the blue," Teller remembered — after lunch at Columbia the previous September: using a fission bomb to set off an even larger nuclear explosion in an isotope of hydrogen, deuterium, which could be extracted cheaply from seawater. The hydrogen reaction would be fusion rather than fission, the heat of the atomic bomb, tens of millions of degrees, imparting such ferocious energy to atoms of deuterium that their nuclei pushed past their mutual electrical repulsion and fused, releasing energy. If a fusion reaction could be lit it would be like lighting a fire; the reaction could be made arbitrarily larger simply by including more deuterium in the bomb. Instead of thousands of tons of TNT equivalence — kilotons — Teller thought a hydrogen bomb might explode with millions of tons of TNT equivalence — megatons. "Edward raised this question...and got everybody interested," Serber remembers. "He'd come in every morning with an agenda, with some bright idea, and then overnight Bethe would prove that it was cockeyed." Serber was supervising atomic-bomb calculations that summer. "They implicitly assumed that I had the fission bomb under control, that there was nothing to worry about." However interesting, the hydrogen bomb was a side issue because it would require a fission bomb to set it off, and such a device hardly existed yet even on paper.

Along the way through these necessary calculations, Oppenheimer realized that a real, physical bomb would have to be designed, built, and somehow tested. Those steps would involve

construction crews up the narrow switchback road to the 7,200-foot mesa to throw together cheap apartment housing. When Serber arrived in March 1943, he remembers, "nothing was organized. Oppy had a tremendous fight with the army to prevent them from cutting down every tree on the whole mesa. He was fairly successful at that."

By the end of March 1943, people could begin moving in. Oppenheimer assigned Serber the job of telling them why they were there. With workmen walking on the roof overhead, Serber began the first of five lectures:

The object of the project is to produce a practical military weapon in the form of a bomb in which the energy is released by a fast neutron chain reaction in one or more of the materials known to show nuclear fission.

Oppenheimer sent Manley forward to interrupt. Don't say "weapon." Manley told Serber. Too many workmen around. "They were worried about security." says Serber. "I should use 'gadget' instead. . . . Around Los Alamos after that we called the bomb we were building the 'gadget.'"

From 1943 until the end of the war, the population crowding onto the narrow mesa doubled every ninety days. Designing the uranium bomb proved to be straightforward. It evolved to a six-foot length of cannon barrel with target rings of U235 screwed into the muzzle; a "bullet" of U235 fired up the barrel mated with the target rings to form a supercritical assembly. The design was inefficient, using some four critical masses, about 60 kilograms of U235, every gram that Groves's gigantic factories were able to squeeze out by July 1945. But it was so conservative that it needed only near-critical testing. Nicknamed "Little Boy," one of a kind, it became the Hiroshima bomb.

Plutonium was a closer call. Since it was notably more unstable than U235, using it in a gun had been problematic from the beginning. Then Emilio Segrè, measuring spontaneous fission in plutonium in a log cabin in a secluded valley away from the mesa, discovered that the plutonium just beginning to come from the production reactors at Hanford was contaminated with an even more active plutonium isotope that would make gun assembly impossible — a bullet of such plutonium, fired up a barrel even at 3,000 feet per second, would melt and vaporize before it reached the target rings. Los Alamos had to invent a new way to assemble a critical mass, or all

explosions, metallurgy, electronics, tricky near-critical assemblies, diagnostics, possibly even a full-scale trial. Oppenheimer proposed establishing a bomb laboratory at an isolated location and Groves agreed. Groves chose Oppenheimer to direct the new laboratory. ("He's a genius," Groves would praise the young theoretician. "A real genius. . . . Why, Oppenheimer knows about everything. He can talk to you about anything you bring up. Well, not exactly. I guess there are a few things he doesn't know about. He doesn't know anything about sports.") They considered Tennessee, looked at sites in Utah and settled on the mesa in New Mexico, due west across the Rio Grande from a primitive ranch high in the Sangre de Christos that Oppenheimer maintained for summer vacations. "My two great loves are physics and desert country," the physicist had written a friend once; "it's a pity they can't be combined." Now they would be.

A boys' school on the mesa gave them a base of buildings and not much else. "What we were trying to do," writes Oppenheimer's assistant John Manley, "was build a new laboratory in the wilds of New Mexico with no initial equipment except the library of Horatio Alger books or whatever it was that those boys in the Ranch School read, and the pack equipment that they used going horseback riding, none of which helped us very much in getting neutron-producing accelerators." Oppenheimer bought a cyclotron from Harvard; Manley scavenged gear from Wisconsin and Berkeley. Groves sent

General Leslie R. Groves and J. Robert Oppenheimer. Washington, D.C., c. September 1945. *Photographer: Unknown. Courtesy of Peter Oppenheimer*

subcritical, at the center of their bomb and squeeze it to criticality. "Fat Man," as they nicknamed the implosion bomb, became a five-foot sphere of nested concentric shells: a walnut-sized initiator at the center to supply a burst of neutrons at the moment of greatest compression; surrounding that, a six-kilogram ball of solid plutonium; surrounding that, a thick spherical "tamper" of natural uranium to reflect neutrons back into the plutonium and hold the explosion together a few millionths of a second longer to allow the chain reaction a longer run; surrounding that, blocks of two different kinds of high explosives cut and fitted together in such a way that the detonation waves that belled from the detonators embedded in the outer blocks would be turned inside out so that they converged inward on the plutonium. The 64 detonators had to fire with millisecond simultaneity; inventive Berkeley physicist Luis Alvarez devised an entirely new electric detonation system that did the job.

Implosion was too complicated to trust to theory. On July 16, 1945, they put it to the test in the high desert south of Albuquerque, a test site Oppenheimer named Trinity in allusion to John Donne's holy sonnet that begins "Batter my heart, three-person'd God. . . ." Everyone who saw the explosion of the first atomic bomb — a Fat Man plutonium implosion bomb without its armored ballistic casing, fired on a hundred-foot tower just before dawn — was awed by the fireball, brighter than the noonday sun, and disturbed by the heat pulse that felt ten miles away as if an oven door had just been opened. When the light faded, physicist I. I. Rabi remembered, "there was an enormous ball of fire which grew and grew and it rolled as it grew; it went up into the air, in yellow flashes and into scarlet and green. It looked menacing. It seemed to come toward one. A new thing had just been born; a new control; a new understanding of man, which man had acquired over nature." After the fireball faded into cloud and washed out with the wind, Rabi adds, "There was a chill, which was not the morning cold; it was a chill that came to one when one thought, as for instance when I thought of my wooden house in Cambridge, and my laboratory in New York, and of the millions of people living around there, and this power of nature which we had first understood it to be — well, there it was."

"Now we are all sons of bitches," Trinity test director Kenneth Bainbridge quipped to Oppenheimer that morning. They had known for more than a year that the Germans had built no atomic bomb, had not even managed a full-scale pile. The bombs they were building were meant for the Japanese. The Japanese had started the

the far-flung efforts of the Manhattan Project would result in only one atomic bomb.

The new method was called implosion. The idea had come up during the Berkeley summer and again in the discussions that followed Serber's lectures, but it had seemed to Oppenheimer a long shot at best. Instead of blowing one piece of plutonium into another, implosion involved wrapping a spherical shell or ball of plutonium with high explosives and somehow timing their detonation so that they squeezed the sphere *inward* to supercriticality. A high-explosive shock wave would travel so much faster than a bullet could be moved that the plutonium should assemble itself before spontaneous fission could cause it to predetonate and fizzle. In the late summer of 1944, the laboratory reorganized itself around the hard problem of making implosion work.

A team of British scientists arrived on the mesa to help, among them an accomplished Soviet spy, the German émigré Klaus Fuchs. One of the British scientists, James Tuck, suggested that the implosion high explosives could be arranged to work as lenses, actually focussing the explosion inward. John von Neumann, the brilliant Hungarian mathematician who was a consultant to the lab, designed the complicated geometry with help from Edward Teller. Teller taught them that explosives could actually compress solid metal to more than double its normal density, forcing the atoms of plutonium closer together. With that fact demonstrated by experiment they decided that they could use a nearly solid ball of plutonium, barely war and had done their share of strategic bombing and mass slaughter in China. They had cruelly mistreated Allied prisoners of war. Their navy and air force were largely destroyed by now, their home islands were blockaded, their cities were undergoing systematic firebombing by the U. S. Army Air Force under Curtis LeMay, but they nevertheless refused to surrender unconditionally as the Allies demanded. How had idealistic physicists come to build weapons of mass destruction? For the time being they were too busy preparing the weapons to ask.

Niels Bohr had visited Los Alamos the previous year after escaping from Nazi-occupied Denmark. Austrian émigré theoretician Victor Weisskopf registers the impact of Bohr's visit:

> *In Los Alamos we were working on something which is perhaps the most questionable, the most problematic thing a scientist can be faced with. At that time physics, our beloved science, was pushed into the most cruel part of reality and we had to live it through . . . . But suddenly in the midst of it, Bohr appeared in Los Alamos.*
>
> *It was the first time we became aware of the sense in all these terrible things, because Bohr right away participated not only in the work, but in our discussions. Every great and deep difficulty bears in itself its own solution. . . . This we learned from him.*

Oppenheimer had recruited them by hinting that the things they would build would end not only the present war but war itself. He hadn't mentioned that they might have to kill tens of thousands of Japanese civilians to achieve that noble goal. Rabi, deeper and harder than Weisskopf, knew that a continuing war in the Pacific would divert shipping that war-ravaged Europe needed to avoid mass starvation. However brutally, the bombs ended the war. Soldiers and sailors staging for the invasion of Japan cheered the news of the first atomic bombings and wept with relief that they would not have to die.

When the news of Hiroshima and Nagasaki reached Los Alamos there was celebration on the mesa, but some were sickened. "You will believe that this undertaking has not been without its misgivings," Oppenheimer wrote a friend soon afterward. To a sunlit outdoor gathering on October 16, 1945, his last day as director, he warned bluntly that "if atomic bombs are to be added as new weapons to the arsenals of a warring world, or to the arsenals of

Oppenheimer's last day as director of the Los Alamos laboratory. October 16, 1945. *Photographer: J.J. Mike Michnovicz. Courtesy of J.J. Mike Michnovicz*

nations preparing for war, then the time will come when mankind will curse the names of Los Alamos and of Hiroshima." Coupling Los Alamos with Hiroshima may seem odd at this distance, when the Japanese city is taken to represent the victim, but Hiroshima was responsible with Los Alamos in supporting and sustaining the war.

The great and deep difficulty of the bomb, Bohr thought, the fact that there was no sure defense against its destructiveness, would force belligerent nations to negotiate together in self-interest to control it; and to do so they would have to open up their political systems to view and to judgment even as they voluntarily denied themselves the power to make war. It didn't work out that way in the short run — nations learn from evidence, not theory, and assurance of national survival takes precedence over issues of morality — but along a different and far more dangerous circuit, by an arms race to mutual deterrence and the balance of terror, it did. The men and women whose photographs appear in this book helped add the knowledge of how to release nuclear energy to the common fund of human experience that we call civilization.

The Photographs

BREAKING GROUND

"MESAS AND MOUNTAINS, RIVERS AND TREES, WINDS AND RAINS ARE AS SENSITIVE TO THE ACTIONS AND THOUGHTS OF HUMANS AS WE ARE TO THEIR FORCES. THEY TAKE INTO THEMSELVES WHAT WE GIVE OFF AND GIVE IT OUT AGAIN." — Edith Warner, in *The House at Otowi Bridge,* by Peggy Pond Church

THE PARAJITO PLATEAU, the Clinch River Valley at Elza, the Jornada del Muerto, the lower Yakima Valley, and Priest Valley Rapids are all places that have been changed irrevocably. These were the lands on which the world's first nuclear weapons were built and tested.

In 1942, Henry L. Stimson, Secretary of War, created the Manhattan Engineering District in accordance with President Roosevelt's orders. Isolated locations across the United States were surveyed, and huge factories, laboratories, and municipalities were quickly built. Condemnation and eviction notices were served to farming communities in the Clinch River Valley of eastern Tennessee in late 1942. The senior boys at the Los Alamos Ranch School, on the Parajito Plateau in north-western New Mexico, were ordered by the army to graduate early in the chilly month of February. The New Mexican state government abruptly terminated the leases of ranchers in the Jornada del Muerto. In 1943, the fruit growers working the irrigated lands of the lower Yakima Valley and Priest Valley Rapids, in the south-central desert of Washington State, received notices to vacate as they were preparing their next crop. Each of these places would soon become known by another name.

Site X, also known as Oak Ridge, or the Clinton Engineering Works, was located in the Clinch River Valley. Like the other project sites, the area was soon to benefit economically from its inclusion in the Manhattan District. Anyone who "had something to sell, trade, lease, loan, or give away," or who wanted a factory job profited. Much of the land was exhausted from generations of farming, but at the time of the eviction notices, when crops were still rising and tobacco curing, some families were given as little as two weeks to leave. Bitter fights ensued over payment for their properties, as the residents disputed the government appraisals. These cases were ultimately resolved in the courts, but for many individuals the psychological dislocation was agonizing.

Site Y, postal address P.O. Box 1663, Santa Fe, high on the Parajito Plateau, was fenced in and a town was built around the now emptied Los Alamos Boys Ranch School. It was Robert Oppenheimer who had suggested a location in New Mexico: physics and the desert both fascinated him. Across the Rio Grande River, the long-time inhabitants of the San Ildefonso Pueblo discovered they had new neighbors.

Site W., named the Hanford Engineering Works, soon reverted to desert after the fruit growers in the valleys of Yakima and the Priest River were evicted. The huge concrete plutonium production plants that rose rapidly there were made from the desert floor itself. The small communities of White Bluffs and Hanford also departed, although moving them was not easy. "These fires had been burning for a hundred and twenty years," a District Colonel later said, "and they [the people] had to be carried out bodily."

Trinity was the code-name for the site and test of the world's first atomic bomb in the Jornada del Muerto — Journey of Death — a part of which was already being used as the Alamogordo Bombing Range by the U.S. Army. Cattle shared the desert with the coyote, the rattlesnakes, and a few ranching families. This remote and primitive land would soon witness the full force of the world's first atomic explosion and be altered as irrevocably as the other Manhattan Project landscapes.

Peach tree.
Oak Ridge, 1942.
Photographer: E. Westcott.
Courtesy of NARA

Otowi Bridge.
Los Alamos, c. 1943.
Photographer: Unknown.
Courtesy of LANL

BIT 38
W MEXICO STATE HIGHWAY NO. 4

Original farmhouse, with construction behind. Oak Ridge, 1942.

Photographer: E. Westcott.
Courtesy of NARA

Hanford Bluffs, 1945.
Photographer: R. Johnson.
Courtesy of the DOE

**Road to Los Alamos,
c. 1945.**
*Photographer: J.J. Mike
Michnovicz.
Courtesy of J.J. Mike
Michnovicz*

Trinity site, 1945.
Photographer: E.
Wallace?
Courtesy of LANL

COLONIZATION

"I HAD ALREADY REALIZED THAT WHEN MY HUSBAND

JOINED THE MANHATTAN PROJECT IT WOULD BE AS IF

WE SHUT A GREAT DOOR BEHIND US. THE WORLD I HAD

KNOWN OF FRIENDS AND FAMILY WOULD NO LONGER BE

REAL TO ME. . . . THE ONLY BRIDGE BETWEEN US

WOULD BE THE SHADOWY ONE OF CENSORED LETTERS.

BY A RAPID TRANSMUTATION, MY HUSBAND AND I HAD

BECOME DIFFERENT PEOPLE. . . . NOW WE WERE PART

OF THE TOP SECRET WAR, THE GREAT SECRET WHICH

LAY BEHIND OUR INNOCENT RURAL ADDRESS. . . ."

— Ruth Marshak, in *Standing By and Making Do,* edited by
Jane S. Wilson and Charlotte Serber

Security gate.
Hanford, c. 1944–45.
Photographer: S.W.
Lewis.
Courtesy of J. Lewis

D URING THE SECOND World War, the most secret laboratories and factories in the United States were built at Sites X, Y, and W. The people who came to live in these secluded installations called their new homes by the names of Oak Ridge, Los Alamos, and Hanford. Beginning early in 1943, thousands of construction workers who passed a simple security clearance were placed on the payroll of the Manhattan District, and put to work building cities surrounded by chain-link fences and patrolled around the clock by the military police.

After the factories had been built, thousands more workers were recruited to join the war effort, accepting jobs whose ultimate goal remained a mystery. At an early stage of the project, General Groves insisted on compartmentalization in all aspects of the Manhattan Project. A worker knew how to perform his or her own task, but nothing more. The work itself was mostly routine and sometimes tedious (though it also posed, for some, radiation dangers they were not told about) but was generally well paid. At Oak Ridge and Hanford, the plants operated around the clock; at Los Alamos, scientists worked a six-day week. I.D. badges were worn at all times; mail was routinely censored, and travel beyond certain boundaries prohibited.

Inside the steel fences, people tried their best to live ordinary lives in extraordinary communities. The army built movie theaters, supermarkets, churches, schools, and baseball diamonds to provide familiar surroundings in these new nuclear towns, but the constant presence of military police and FBI agents reminded the population that the trappings of normality only masked a strange reality.

At Oak Ridge (Site X), alongside the administrative headquarters of the Manhattan District, large factories were built to fuel the bomb. Life in Oak Ridge was not unlike that in frontier boomtowns of the nineteenth century: no sidewalks meant mud in the spring and dust in the summer. Houses were erected in the blink of an eye (the busiest month saw 1,000 finished), stores were half-stocked, telephones virtually non-existent. In 1942, the original projection for the town was 13,000 people; 42,000 lived there by 1944, and in 1945 the population reached its peak of 75,000 as the plants attained a full operating schedule. This "instant" city became Tennessee's fifth largest. By 1945, the army had built 10,000 family units, 13,000 dormitory spaces, 16,000 hutments and barracks, and 5,000 trailers. The first families arrived in the summer of 1943. The town had been built so quickly and so secretly, however, that no house possessed an official address.

A company was formed to manage the town for the army. The Roane-Anderson corporation maintained the schools, ran theaters, bowling alleys, bars and libraries, and published a weekly newspaper. It delivered coal in the winter and ice in the summer, and it operated a bus service over the several miles separating the nuclear plants from residential areas.

At Hanford (Site W), giant factories for processing plutonium were built, but because of the dangers of radioactivity, 17,000 operating personnel, scientists, engineers, and military personnel were housed in Richland, twenty miles from the plant. Pre-fabricated housing, complete with furniture, was hauled to this small town. Closer to the plant was a construction camp intended to house only two thousand workers; at its peak, the camp had to accommodate 45,000. Discontent abounded, especially in the construction camp — individuals felt isolated, husbands and wives were not permitted to live together, and families were discouraged from coming at all. Dust storms plagued everyone. Understandably, worker turnover was high. The official photographer at Hanford, Robley Johnson, estimated that he made over 145,000 identification photographs for this revolving-door population. The army soon recognized that the question of worker morale had to be addressed. Thus, in a change of policy, families were permitted to live together in trailer camps, a tent movie theater was built, various sport facilities were erected, and an order came down directly from General Groves that beer was to be sold in any quantity.

At Los Alamos (Site Y), the scenery was spectacular, but the hastily-built housing and basic laboratory facilities diminished some of the splendor. "The rickety houses looked like the tenements of a metropolitan slum area," one resident reminisced, "washing hung everywhere, and the garbage cans were overflowing." On this mesa, the first atomic bombs would be designed and built. Scientists were persuaded or cajoled by the newly-appointed director of the laboratory, Robert Oppenheimer, to come and join him on a particular kind of scientific endeavor in a town that was not marked on any map. Originally conceived as a laboratory of 400 scientists, Los Alamos eventually housed nearly 7,000. Security was strictest at Los Alamos and, for the European émigré scientists who had themselves recently fled totalitarian regimes, was a bitter pill to swallow. One Los Alamos resident remembered that the fence ". . . was a tangible barrier, a symbol of our isolated lives." However, the fence had at least one gap through which several children moved secretly between the world of the Manhattan Project and that beyond.

Page from Military
Police identification
book.
Los Alamos, 1943.
Photographer: Unknown.
Courtesy of LANL

Military security and its restrictions were a fact of life in the
Manhattan District. All personnel were subject to a security check
or clearance, depending on the sensitivity of their work. Everyone
was fingerprinted and wore an I.D. badge. Key scientists had their
names changed and kept bodyguards in tow.

Sergeant, with
guard tower in the
background.
Oak Ridge, 1945.
Photographer E. Westcott.
Courtesy of NARA

Top left:

Oak Ridge, 1943.

Photographer: E. Westcott.

Courtesy of NARA

Bottom left:

Construction camp. Hanford, 1944.

Photographer: R. Johnson.

Courtesy of the DOE

Top right:

Oak Ridge, 1944.

Photographer: A. Milch.

Courtesy of A. Milch

Bottom right:

Los Alamos housing, 1943.

Photographer: C. Crumb.

Courtesy of C. Crumb

Since construction of all three towns took place hurriedly, the army had to continually revise its population figures. Bernice Brode, the wife of a Los Alamos physicist, wrote: "In the next years I was to learn that the army could maintain this bulldozing momentum . . . replacing strata of timeless growth with ugly buildings whose purpose was not beauty but grim utility." Living

conditions were sometimes rough: there were no paved roads, and Oak Ridge and Los Alamos were almost constantly covered in mud. At Hanford, dust blew in under closed doors, forming small dunes in living rooms and kitchens overnight.

Top left:
Unloading trailer homes.
Oak Ridge, 1943.
Photographer E. Westcott.
Courtesy of NARA

Bottom left:
New housing.
Hanford, c. 1944.
Photographer: S.W. Lewis.
Courtesy of J. Lewis

Top right:
Hutments.
Los Alamos, 1945.
Photographer: J.J. Mike Michnovicz.
Courtesy of J.J. Mike Michnovicz

Bottom right:
Pre-fabricated house.
Oak Ridge, c. 1944.
Photographer: E. Westcott.
Courtesy of NARA

Public relations photography was used both to recruit new employees and to raise the morale of workers and their families. Staff reporters covered stories much like those of any small town, but with a significant difference. The *Oak Ridge Journal's* by-line read: "NOT TO BE TAKEN OR MAILED FROM THE AREA" and the *Hanford Sage Sentinel* instructed readers that "The Information contained in this publication shall not be communicated to the public or press."

Top left:
Hanford, c. 1944.
Photographer: R. Johnson.
Courtesy of the DOE

Bottom left:
Oak Ridge, c. 1944.
Photographer: E. Westcott.
Courtesy of NARA

Top right:
Hanford, c. 1944.
Photographer: R. Johnson.
Courtesy of the DOE

Bottom right:
Hanford, c. 1944.
Photographer: R. Johnson.
Courtesy of the DOE

Oak Ridge, c. 1944.
Photographer: E. Westcott.
Courtesy of NARA

Oak Ridge, c. 1944.
Photographer: E.
Westcott.
Courtesy of NARA

Excerpt from a Hanford recruitment brochure:

Should I Bring My Family?

Unless you have your own trailer, it is almost impossible to find living quarters for a family. There are no trailers or houses for rent in Hanford and no accommodations for married couples to live together in the barracks. Conditions in nearby towns are crowded. But if you do have a trailer, you may rent space, water, electricity, and the use of a bathhouse for $3 a week.

Hanford, c. 1944.
Photographer: R. Johnson.
Courtesy of the DOE

Oak Ridge, c. 1944.
Photographer: E.
Westcott.
Courtesy of NARA

General Leslie Groves had just completed the construction of the Pentagon when he reluctantly accepted command of the Manhattan District in September 1942. He replaced Colonel James Marshall, whose offices were in New York City — hence the project's code name: Manhattan. Oak Ridge became the administrative headquarters (the offices were nicknamed the "Castle"), but Groves retained his personal office in Washington, D.C., closer to the heart of political power.

A Special Engineer Detachment (SED) was formed by the Army Corps of Engineers to retain young technicians and scientists otherwise bound for overseas. Recently organized WAC (Women's Army Corps) detachments were also dispatched to the three sites. They handled the clerical work, which Groves felt required strict military control.

The physicists who followed Oppenheimer to Los Alamos were recruited from leading American universities or had held distinguished positions abroad. The scientists had difficulty accepting the authoritarian ways of the army: Groves' suggestion that the scientists be put in uniform, for instance, was unacceptable to them, despite Oppenheimer's support.

The residents of Los Alamos tried to lead ordinary lives. On their day off, the physicists, chemists, engineers, and mathematicians could be found hiking or skiing in the hills surrounding Los Alamos. Some visited Edith Warner, who lived below the mesa by Otowi Bridge. She was the link between the Anglo and Pueblo civilizations. Edith and her companion, Tilano, ran a tea room and occasionally entertained selected scientists. After the war, when the laboratory was expanded, Pueblo Indians and scientists, working together, built her a new home, away from the road.

Top, left to right:

Enrico Fermi (physicist and Associate Director of the Los Alamos laboratory).
Redondo, 1945.
Photographer: Donald W. Kerst.
Courtesy of Dorothy Kerst

Louis Hempelmann (health physicist) in front of an old Ranch School Building.
Los Alamos, 1945.
Photographer: N. Metropolis.
Courtesy of N. Metropolis

Edith Warner and Tilano in front of their house at Otowi Bridge. Los Alamos, January, 1945.
Photographer: L.D.P. King.
Courtesy of L.D.P. King

Bottom, left to right:

Françoise and Stanislaw Ulam (mathematician). Los Alamos, 1945.
Photographer: N. Metropolis.
Courtesy of N. Metropolis

William Penney (experimental physicist), Emil Konopinski (theoretical physicist), Beatrice and Lawrence Langer (experimental physicist), holding a puppy named Gadget. Los Alamos, 1944.
Photographer: N. Metropolis.
Courtesy of N. Metropolis

Richard Feynman (theoretical physicist). Frijoles, c. 1945.
Photographer: N. Metropolis.
Courtesy of N. Metropolis

Left from top:

Enrico Fermi, Rose and Hans Bethe (theoretical physicist), with the King family on a picnic at Nabe Lake, c. 1945.
Photographer: L.D.P. King.
Courtesy of L.D.P. King

Joan Hinton (experimental physicist), Darragh Nagle (experimental physicist), and George Kistiakowsky (chemist), skiing. Los Alamos, c. 1945.
Photographer: L.D.P. King.
Courtesy of L.D.P. King

Center from top:

Bruno Rossi (experimental physicist). Jemez Mountains, 1945.
Photographer: Donald W. Kerst.
Courtesy of Dorothy B. Kerst

Earl Long (chemist), Enrico and his daughter Nella Fermi. Lake Peak, c. 1945.
Photographer: L.D.P. King.
Courtesy of L.D.P. King

Elizabeth Graves (physicist), Philip Morrison (experimental physicist), Edith Warner, and Edith King (wife of experimental physicist L.D.P. King), at a picnic lunch. Los Alamos, c. 1946.
Photographer: L.D.P. King.
Courtesy of L.D.P. King

Below:
Building Edith Warner's new home at Otowi Bridge. Los Alamos, June 1947.
Photographer: L.D.P. King.
Courtesy of L.D.P. King

Top and bottom:

Barbed wire fences separated the atomic projects from the surrounding countryside. Hanford, 1944.

Photographer: R. Johnson.

Courtesy of the DOE

Opposite:

Physicists Leona Woods and John Marshall met at the University of Chicago while helping Enrico Fermi construct the first atomic pile. They married and took their newborn son Peter with them to Hanford to work on the first industrial nuclear reactors.

Leona, John, and Peter Marshall in Richland Village. Hanford, 1944–1945.
Photographer: John Marshall and Leona Marshall Libby. Courtesy of J. Marshall

A schoolroom.
Oak Ridge, 1944.
Photographer: E.
Westcott.
Courtesy of NARA

Many children were born within the confines of the three secret towns during the war years. At Los Alamos, General Groves grumbled to Oppenheimer about what one resident called "the wholesale quantity of babies," and inspired this jingle:

> *The General's in a stew*
> *He trusted you and you*
> *He thought you'd be scientific*
> *Instead you're just prolific*
> *And what is he to do?*

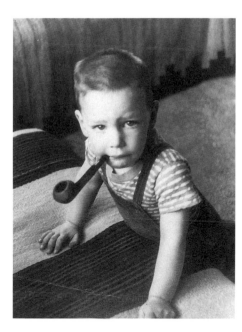

Above:
Paul Teller, three years old, on the shoulders of his father Edward Teller (theoretical physicist), at a conference with Julian Schwinger and David Inglis.
Los Alamos, 1946.
Photographer: J.J. Mike Michnovicz.
Courtesy of J.J. Mike Michnovicz

From left: / *Courtesy of the J. Robert Oppenheimer Memorial Committee*

Peter Oppenheimer, two years old, with his father's pipe.
Los Alamos, 1943.
Photographer: K. Oppenheimer.

Steven Kolodney, two years old, at Ashley Pond. The Technical Area laboratories, off-limits to non-scientists, are seen in the background.
Los Alamos, 1943.

Photographer: M. Kolodney.
Courtesy of M. Kolodney

Kim and Kathy Manley, the daughters of Kay and John Manley (physicist and Oppenheimer's assistant), inside their "bathtub row" home, which dated from the time of the Los Alamos Boys Ranch School.
Los Alamos, c. 1944.
Photographer: J.J. Mike Michnovicz.
Courtesy of J.J. Mike Michnovicz

Edward Teller leaving
Chicago on his way to
Los Alamos, 1943.
Photographer: Leona
Marshall Libby.
Courtesy of J. Marshall

Niels Bohr skiing
on Sawyer's Hill.
Los Alamos, 1944.

Photographer: Becky
Diven.
Courtesy of Nella Fermi
Weiner

Naomi French
(mathematician),
Joshua tree, and car.
Anthony French
(a member of the
British Mission) and
his wife Naomi
purchased the car
Klaus Fuchs had used
to meet his Soviet
courier in Santa Fe.
Arizona, 1946.
Photographer: A. French.
Courtesy of Anthony and
Naomi French

Many of the scientists who worked on the Manhattan Project were European-born. Some, like Edward Teller, left their homeland before the war to escape fascism and rising anti-semitism; others came later as wartime refugees. In December 1943, the British Mission, under the leadership of Nobel-prize winner James Chadwick, arrived in Los Alamos. The eminent Danish physicist Niels Bohr also came as a consultant to Los Alamos several times. Bohr had escaped Nazi-occupied Denmark in 1943 and was an advisor to the British government on scientific matters. One of the architects of atomic theory, Bohr now found many of his old stu-dents at Los Alamos, where he was known by the code-name Nicholas Baker. Bohr's presence was not merely beneficial to research: he also had a profound effect on the laboratory's morale, and influenced Oppenheimer's thinking about atomic weapons. Bohr was one of the first to think about the probability of an arms race with Russia. What he did not know was that the race had already begun — Klaus Fuchs, a valued member of the British Mission, was already supplying critical scientific information to the Russians.

Pantomime at a party hosted by the British Mission after the war. Los Alamos, September 1945.
Photographer: J.J. Mike Michnovicz.
Courtesy of J.J. Mike Michnovicz

The artificially small world of Los Alamos was permeated by social stratification. The scientific community had its own tensions: "We were too many of one kind, all packed together. We could not unburden our souls by bringing our complaints to outsiders; they had to remain either within ourselves or within the community," Laura Fermi remembered. European and American-born scientists tended to socialize separately, and a wide gulf existed between the "long-hairs," as General Groves called the scientists, and the military. SEDs bridged the gap — although they were in uniform, their training brought them into the scientific community.

Dorothy McKibbin, Robert Oppenheimer, and Victor Weisskopf at a party. Los Alamos, c. 1945.
Photographer: Unknown. Courtesy of LANL

Top left, right:

Jeanne Crumb (wife of SED Carl Crumb), entering her home.
Los Alamos, 1946.
Photographer: C. Crumb.
Courtesy of C. Crumb

Berenice Vickio (nurse), and Mike Vickio (military police).
Los Alamos, 1946.
Photographer: C. Crumb.
Courtesy of C. Crumb

Bottom left, right:

SED Al Hershey outside the men's barracks.
Los Alamos, 1944.
Photographer: C. Crumb.
Courtesy of C. Crumb

SED barracks interior from top bunk.
Los Alamos, 1944.
Photographer: C. Crumb.
Courtesy of C. Crumb

Jackson Square
shopping center.
Oak Ridge, 1944.
Photographer: E. Westcott.
Courtesy of NARA

Bottom left:
Barracks interior.
Hanford, December
1943.

Photographer: R.
Johnson.
Courtesy of the DOE

Housing was one of the main complaints at Los Alamos and many disputes among the scientists were aired at the tiny housing office run for a time by Rose Bethe. Homes were allocated according to family size, but exceptions were certainly made. Rent was paid according to one's salary, and one's salary was based strictly on what one had earned before arriving at Los Alamos. Thus, some construction men earned more than some scientists.

At Hanford and Oak Ridge, housing was allocated according to the job. Unskilled workers lived in hutments, while plant managers were given pre-fabricated homes. During construction at Hanford, men and women lived in separate barracks divided by high fences.

Men's barracks room.
Hanford, January
1945.
Photographer: R.
Johnson.
Courtesy of the DOE

Apartment house
interior.
Los Alamos, c. 1945.
Photographer: Unknown.
Courtesy of LANL

Several Indian Pueblos surrounded Los Alamos. When the army arrived to build the laboratory, domestic servants were recruited so that the wives of the physicists could work on the Project. Construction crews also hired Pueblo Indians and Spanish-Americans for numerous projects.

The encounter made an impression on both groups: soon running water and electrical cables were installed in the San Ildefonso Pueblo by some scientists; some of the Los Alamos residents occasionally attended weddings and rituals. Bernice Brode wondered, though, whether the Indian dances she watched had been especially created for outsiders such as herself.

Bingo night.
Hanford, 1944.
Photographer: R. Johnson.
Courtesy of the DOE

Opposite, from top:

Movie theater in Pasco,
near Hanford, 1943.
Photographer: R. Johnson.
Courtesy of the DOE

Bank lines.
Hanford, 1944.
Photographer: R. Johnson.
Courtesy of the DOE

Opposite, far right,
from top:

Incident.
Hanford, c. 1944.
Photographer: S.W. Lewis.
Courtesy of J. Lewis

Stabbing victim.
Hanford, c. 1944.
Photographer: S.W. Lewis.
Courtesy of J. Lewis

Hanford was a tough town. Anyone who hadn't been previously arrested or had his license suspended, could be hired on the construction crew. Weekends were often wild: "There was nothing to do except fight, with the result that occasionally bodies were found in garbage cans the next morning," Leona Woods Marshall recalled. The beer hall was also popular. Jerry Saucier, an inspector, remembered: "They had some big games . . . They'd put their week's check down, and boy, that was their fun." Between March 1943 and August 1944, the police recorded 3,156 incidents of drunkenness, 1,124 burglaries, 522 assaults, five violent deaths, and four suicides.

Segregated living arrangements existed during the war years in Oak Ridge. The hutments allocated to the 1,500 member black population at Oak Ridge had dirt floors, coal stoves, and no glass windows. Black married couples could not live together until after the war, and there were no schools for their children until 1946. The hutments were separated by a fence within a fence so that members of the white community were hardly aware a "Negro Village" existed at all.

**Interior of pre-fabri-
cated housing.
Oak Ridge, 1945.**
*Photographer: E. Westcott.
Courtesy of NARA*

**Exterior,
"Negro Hutments."
Oak Ridge, 1945.**
*Photographer: E. Westcott.
Courtesy of NARA*

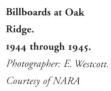

After the war ended, the towns of Oak Ridge, Hanford, and Los Alamos remained in a state of limbo until the newly-formed Atomic Energy Commission replaced the Manhattan Engineering District on January 1, 1947. Many left the secret cities to return to their ordinary lives. The towns themselves, however, remained closed to outsiders.

Oak Ridge was opened to the public in 1949; at Hanford, the residents of Richland were finally able to purchase their homes in 1956; and a year later, the gates at the east and west entrances to Los Alamos were finally opened. A vacant guard tower remains there to this day.

Celebration of the
Japanese surrender.
(Tojo was the former
Prime Minister of
Japan.)
Oak Ridge,
August 14, 1945.
Photographer: E.
Westcott.
Courtesy of NARA

The Manhattan Project Atomic Bomb Investigating Group
(made up of scientists and doctors from Los Alamos and Oak
Ridge) was sent to Japan in August 1945 to survey the effects of
the two atomic bombs, and to measure radiation levels in
Hiroshima and Nagasaki before the first American ground troops
were permitted entrance.

Manhattan District doctor Henry Barnett with two Japanese nurses.
Nagasaki, September–October 1945.
Photographer: Unknown
Courtesy of Henry Barnett

The Mayor of Nagasaki with the Manhattan Project Atomic Bomb Investigating Group.
September–October, 1945.
Photographer: Unknown
Courtesy of Robert Serber

After the Manhattan Project group had made preliminary inspections, the Governor of Nagasaki held a banquet for the small scientific team in the red light district of the city, one of the few areas undamaged by the bomb. Because the Admiral of the U.S. Navy, however, had declared the section off-limits to American servicemen, the Military Police burst in to break up a party they

BOHR AND WHEELER BELIEVED, CORRECTLY, THAT ONLY A PARTICULARLY RARE VARIETY OF URANIUM COULD BE USED EFFECTIVELY IN THE CREATION OF AN ATOMIC EXPLOSION. BOHR SAID THIS RARE VARIETY COULD NOT BE SEPARATED FROM COMMON URANIUM EXCEPT BY TURNING THE COUNTRY INTO A GIGANTIC FACTORY. . . . YEARS LATER, WHEN BOHR CAME TO LOS ALAMOS, I WAS PREPARED TO SAY, "YOU SEE . . ." BUT BEFORE I COULD OPEN MY MOUTH, HE SAID: "YOU SEE, I TOLD YOU IT COULDN'T BE DONE WITHOUT TURNING THE WHOLE COUNTRY INTO A FACTORY. YOU HAVE DONE JUST THAT." — *The Legacy of Hiroshima,* by Edward Teller

FUEL

URANIUM-235 DESTROYED Hiroshima. Plutonium-239 devastated Nagasaki. These elements, which were the only ones that could be used to make atomic bombs, were manufactured in enormous industrial complexes that painstakingly produced, drop by drop and gram by gram, the fissile material necessary for their fuel. It was the single most difficult task of the Manhattan Project.

The possibility of making an atomic bomb depended not only upon using an element that could be broken up to release the enormous energy stored in its nuclei, but upon utilizing one whose atoms would continue on their own to blow themselves apart. An explosion equivalent to that of thousands of tons of TNT might be produced from a mass the size of a grapefruit. Finding this element initially was not that difficult: uranium could be mined from the earth's crust, but only its lighter isotope, uranium-235 was fissionable, and it made up less than one percent of naturally occurring uranium. The only means of separation was according to their slightly differing weight, since the isotopes' shared chemistry precludes chemical separation. This process of enrichment was a formidable challenge.

By 1941 physicists had also discovered that the remaining 99% of uranium-238, instead of undergoing fission by neutrons, absorbed them and was transmuted into an element they called plutonium. In a nuclear reactor, which uses uranium as its fuel, plutonium is formed. It was thought that the new element would be easier to produce than uranium-235 because it could be chemically separated from uranium. It became the second fuel manufactured by the Manhattan Engineering District for the bomb.

Almost every industrialized country in the world had sufficient information to initiate some sort of atomic bomb project before the Second World War broke out, but only the United States had both the industrial resources and the manpower to launch the mammoth effort involved during the war itself. This, combined with the collective brilliance of native and émigré scientists, gave the Americans a critical advantage in constructing the bomb. Despite this advantage, no efficient means existed to produce useful amounts of either uranium-235 or plutonium when General Groves took command of the Manhattan Project in 1942. At this time, all experimental production methods were based upon laboratory-scale techniques, which could produce only minute quantities of the necessary materials. It was clear to Groves that a huge engineering effort would be necessary if sufficient quantities of fuel were to be generated. Therefore, the general persuaded almost every major American industrial or chemical firm to help in designing and building the massive production factories for the Manhattan District. The scientists did the basic research in physics and chemistry, but it was the engineers who made the production of the bombs' active cores possible.

The uranium enrichment factories were built at Oak Ridge, Tennessee. The army had decided to gamble on three distinct methods of producing bomb-grade uranium, as there was no certainty in 1942 about which method — gaseous diffusion, electromagnetic separation, or thermal diffusion — would be the most efficient. Three huge industrial complexes were hurriedly built and all were used to produce uranium-235. A pilot nuclear reactor was also erected at Oak Ridge as a small-scale version of the plutonium production piles and chemical separation processes at Hanford in Washington State.

Hanford was devoted entirely to the production of plutonium and was the largest single construction project undertaken anywhere in the United States during the entire war. In just eighteen months, designs for the mass production of plutonium were created, the first reactor was built and made operational, and two other reactors and three chemical separation plants were also assembled. Laboratories, workshops, storage tanks, holding basins, and sewers were built, while hundreds of miles of roads, railway tracks, and pipes were laid. Designs had to be modified on the factory floor instead of on blueprints because of the race against time to produce the bomb.

The physical product of these massive nuclear factories, small amounts of plutonium 239 and uranium 235, were made by tens of thousands of workers in Hanford and Oak Ridge. Carefully transported to Los Alamos, these materials were made into solid metal, essential for the bomb's core, by a mere handful of scientists at the Los Alamos laboratory.

When news that the atomic bombs had been dropped on Hiroshima and Nagasaki was broadcast many months later, some of those most surprised were the very people who had helped build them. Groves's policy of compartmentalization ensured that only a handful of people at Oak Ridge and Hanford knew exactly what was being made and why. Workers at both plants had been puzzled by the vast quantities of materials going in when nothing apparently came out. They had no idea that the world's largest array of industrial technology existed only to generate a few pounds of uranium and plutonium. They also didn't know that those few pounds would soon ravage entire cities and their inhabitants.

Hanford was built and operated by the Du Pont Company of Wilmington, Delaware. Its president was asked personally by General Groves to assume production of plutonium even before the scientific feasibility of the atomic bomb had been established by demonstrating a chain reaction. The chemical company received one dollar in payment from the army for its services, but insisted that the government cover it from any liability with a twenty million dollar insurance policy.

Construction of the world's first large scale nuclear reactors began before their designs had been completed. They were built solely to make plutonium; the energy produced was a byproduct. Eugene Wigner and his group at the Met Lab in Chicago created the basic design, which was based on Enrico Fermi's chain-reacting pile of graphite and uranium. Du Pont was responsible for the actual engineering work, and sent the blueprints to Wigner's group for review. There was friction between the scientists at Chicago and the engineers at Du Pont. The scientists, who knew the ultimate goal of their work, and who were worried that the Germans were far ahead of them, felt that any delays caused by instructing engineers in nuclear physics were a waste of precious time. However, the contributions of the engineers would ultimately prove invaluable.

Beads of liquid plutonium metal forming on a cathode (cathode diameter = 1 mm; cathode bead diameter = 3mm). Los Alamos, May 1944.
Photographer: M. Kolodney.
Courtesy of M. Kolodney

100 **F area, plutonium-producing reactor at right. Hanford, 1944.**

Photographer: R. Johnson. Courtesy of the DOE

Three plutonium-producing reactors were built along the Columbia River, five miles apart. At each **site, in addition to the reactor buildings, there were electrical substations, pump stations, water** **treatment plants, retention basins, and waste processing plants.**

The nuclear reactors had to be fueled in order to produce plutonium. Uranium-238 was formed into metal for insertion into the reactor, but the metal itself behaved strangely. A small research program at the Ames Laboratory of Iowa State College was established to conduct metallurgical research. The group developed a method of mass-producing uranium-238 metal of exceptionally high purity, and created a large-scale metal casting. Over two million bars of uranium-238 metal were produced in Iowa to fuel the reactors, before larger industrial-scale methods were operating in Detroit at the Wolverine Tube Company.

The uranium-238 metal billets were extruded into rods. At Hanford the rods were then machined into short slugs for insertion into the reactor.

Ames Laboratory. Iowa, c. 1943. *Photographer: Robert P. Smith? Courtesy of Ames Laboratory*

Interior of a furnace, where uranium-238 metal cools inside a reduction vessel after firing.

Ames Laboratory. Iowa, c. 1943. *Photographer: Robert P. Smith? Courtesy of Ames Laboratory*

Front face of the plutonium-producing reactor in the 100 F area.
Hanford, February 1945.

Photographer: R. Johnson.
Courtesy of the DOE

Uranium-238 metal fuel slugs were inserted horizontally into the front face of a graphite cube $37 \times 46 \times 41$ feet. Water cooled the reactor, which was designed to run at 250 megawatt power. Twenty-seven safety rods stopped the chain reaction by absorbing neutrons when the critical mass of uranium slugs was in place. Other control rods were slotted into the graphite so that operators could control the reactor's power.

Hanford's first reactor went critical a few minutes after midnight on September 26, 1944. Then it shut itself down. A few hours later it regained reactivity. Physicist John Wheeler won a race with Fermi, who was also present, to determine what had happened. It appeared that a fission by-product, iodine-135, was being produced. After a few hours it decayed into xenon-135. The xenon absorbed so many neutrons it halted the chain reaction until it decayed into a non-neutron absorbing element. Then the chain reaction could begin again. Because a Du Pont engineer had earlier insisted on adding extra fuel assemblies (that had delayed construction and cost the army additional millions), the xenon poisoning was eradicated. All three reactors were fully operational by the end of 1944.

Concrete front face of
the experimental
nuclear reactor, X-10.
Oak Ridge, 1943.
Photographer: E.
Westcott.
Courtesy of NARA

X-10 was the code-
name given to the
reactor built by Du
Pont at Oak Ridge.
This air-cooled reactor
had been initially
planned as a prototype
for Hanford's industri-
al-scale reactors.
However, when
Eugene Wigner
changed the designs to
a water-cooled system,
the construction of
X-10 was almost com-
plete. X-10 went criti-
cal at 5:00 AM on
November 4, 1943.
The reactor was put to
use immediately and,
by the end of the year,
had produced 1.54
milligrams of plutoni-
um that was much
needed by the Los
Alamos scientists.
X-10 tested Hanford's
plutonium separation
process, and was used
to study radioactive
isotopes which, imme-
diately after the war,
were used in medicine.

**Neptunium peroxide.
University of Chicago,
September 30, 1943.**
*Photographer: Unknown.
Courtesy of Lawrence
Berkeley Laboratory*

When uranium-238 — the heavier isotope of uranium — absorbs neutrons, it transmutes into neptunium which, being extremely unstable, decays after several days into plutonium: from two tons of irradiated uranium, however, only approximately a dime's volume of the strange new element was produced. Research was consolidated at the Met Lab in 1942, where a chemical method for extracting plutonium from irradiated uranium-238 slugs was devised on a small scale.

Top and bottom:

Separation buildings

under construction.

Hanford, 1944.

Photographer: R.
Johnson.

Courtesy of the DOE

P 7283

The scale of the ultramicrochemistry work at Chicago was increased by a factor of a million at Hanford. Two huge chemical separation plants were built and nicknamed "Queen Marys" after the famous ocean liner. A third plant was a mock-up unit: every installation procedure and piece of equipment was tested here first. A unique system of periscopes and the very first American television sets were installed in the process areas in order to allow operation by remote control. This system was implemented because the process areas became too radioactive for repair crews to enter. The main separation building was called a canyon, and was divided into forty separate cells. A maze of pipes and valves connected one cell to another. The operating gallery lay behind a seven-foot-thick concrete wall.

Completed "Queen Mary," in the 200-west area. A plutonium-producing reactor can be seen on the horizon at right.

Hanford, September 1944.
Photographer: R. Johnson.
Courtesy of the DOE

Rail cars brought the irradiated uranium slugs (which had been pushed out the back of the reactor), to the separation area in large vats of water. Here, they were stored in pools of water for several days while the intense, heat-producing short-lived radioactivity of the fission products decayed.

P 6147

SECRET

Cell interior with process equipment. Hanford, 1945.
Photographer: R. Johnson.
Courtesy of the DOE

The slugs were dissolved in nitric acid and the liquid moved through stage after stage of processing equipment in each cell of the canyon. Because the plutonium became more concentrated at each stage, progressively smaller equipment had to be designed so that the possibility of an accidental critical mass could be eliminated.

SECRET   D 7501

Operating gallery, 221 B building. Hanford, February 1945.

Photographer: R. Johnson. Courtesy of the DOE

Construction of
underground liquid
waste storage tanks
at the 200 C area.
Hanford, c. 1943.

Photographer: R.
Johnson.
Courtesy of the DOE

At the end of the chemical separation process, after a few grams of plutonium nitrate had been extracted, a large amount of waste material had to be disposed of. Much of it was still radioactive. Waste disposal methods were an issue that the Manhattan Project never fully addressed. Sixteen underground waste storage tanks, twelve of which were seventy-five feet in diameter, were built at each plant. They were never intended for long-term storage, although they are still in existence today. The tanks were constructed of reinforced concrete with a steel lining and an air cooler, which turned the vapor produced by the heat of the waste back into a liquid. Despite these precautions, the tanks began leaking dangerous waste into the soil even before the Manhattan Project had officially ended.

Waste tank.
Hanford, 1943.
Photographer: R.
Johnson.
Courtesy of the DOE

Although separating plutonium was difficult, it could at least be done chemically. Enriching uranium had to be done physically, separating atom by atom the fissionable isotope uranium-235 from the heavier isotope, uranium-238. Only approximately one part in 140 was uranium-235, and at least several pounds of uranium-235 would be needed for a single bomb.

K-25 was the code-name given to the largest industrial complex built at Oak Ridge, to separate uranium by gaseous diffusion. The plant was two miles around, occupied forty-four acres, employed 12,000 people, and absorbed a quarter of the Manhattan Project's two billion dollar budget. The gaseous diffusion separation method was based on the principle that when uranium is turned into a gaseous compound (uranium hexaflouride) and passed through a barrier, the heavier isotopes move more slowly and are left behind. Despite the simplicity of this idea, the engineering problems were immense.

The converted uranium hexafluoride gas was extremely corrosive and destroyed ordinary pipes, filters, and pumps. All of the K-25 plant equipment had to be designed specifically to prevent this corrosion from occurring. Vacuum-sealed chambers were made both to prevent the gas from contaminating the delicate equipment and to prevent air from blocking the porous filter barriers. Since so little enrichment of uranium-235 occurred at each barrier, many thousands of thin mesh barriers were installed for the gas to pass through many thousands of times. This was the cascade assembly, which was built on the first floor of the plant. On the second floor, inspection crews checked the miles of pipes, cables, and valves that connected the chambers. Operation of the plant itself was conducted from the third floor. K-25, which was built by the J.A. Jones Company of Charlotte, North Carolina, and operated by Union Carbide, was the largest, fully automated plant built in the United States at that time.

The K-25 plant under construction. Oak Ridge, June 1944.
Photographer: E. Westcott.
Courtesy of NARA

Air was constantly being filtered inside K-25, as a violent reaction would occur if the uranium hexafluoride gas came into contact with grease or oil during operation. As the plant was being built, maintenance crews continuously cleaned and vacuumed the construction areas to ensure that nothing would pollute the system. Even delivery trucks were hosed down before entering the plant.

Ventilators on the roof of the gaseous diffusion plant. Oak Ridge, April 1945. *Photographer: E. Westcott. Courtesy of NARA*

The Linde Air Products Division, an affiliate of Union Carbide, supplied uranium oxide, made from ore, for the Manhattan District. Two plants, with 168 workers, operated in the small town of Tonawanda, near Niagara Falls, New York. In the 1980s, it was revealed that 37 million gallons of radioactive waste had been dumped in shallow wells at Tonawanda by Linde and the army. Radioactive waste from the Manhattan District was also dumped in Lewiston (north of Niagara Falls) and buried at Love Canal (north of Tonawanda).
Photographer: Unknown. Courtesy of NARA

The heart of the gaseous diffusion process was the barrier. Its production was the most intractable of K-25's problems and had worried General Groves to such an extent that he considered eliminating the factory altogether. The barrier material had to consist of millions of tiny holes less than a millionth of an inch wide and yet be strong enough to withstand industrial scale production and corrosive operating conditions. Hundreds of different types were tested. Houdaille-Hershey, a company that used nickel to plate automobile bumpers, built a five-million-dollar plant based on one design that later had to be abandoned. This expensive plant was then completely dismantled, and refitted to accommodate a newly-adopted barrier.
Photographer: Unknown. Courtesy of Decatur *(Illinois)* Herald and Review/*Decatur Public Library*

Much of the uranium production for the Manhattan District was handled by the United States Vanadium Corporation, which had plants in Uraven, Durango, Grand Junction, Montrose, and Rifle, Colorado. 3,000 people were employed to mine and process uranium.
Photographer: Unknown. Courtesy of NARA

One of the last interior cell structures built in the K-25 plant, awaiting equipment installation.

Oak Ridge, February 1945.
Photographer: E. Westcott.
Courtesy of *NARA*

Switch yard for K-25 plant.
Oak Ridge, December 1945.

Photographer: E. Westcott. Courtesy of NARA

An independent power plant to supply K-25 with sufficient power to light the entire city of Boston was built. Because of uncertainty about the frequency requirements of the yet-to-be-designed equipment, the plant was built to accomodate five separate frequencies. This means of solving a problem was typical of the Manhattan Project. So was Groves's fear of sabotage: he had all the cables laid underground.

A master control room for leak detection at K-25.
Oak Ridge, May 1945.

Photographer: E. Westcott. Courtesy of NARA

The tiniest leak in any of the hundreds of miles of pipes, valves, joints or weldings could have damaged the 500 million dollar plant irretrievably. In order to detect microscopic leaks, a portable mass spectrometer was adapted by physicist Alfred O. Nier, and produced in large numbers by General Electric. The spectrometers checked the composition of the hexafluoride gas at any given point so that even a molecule-sized leak could be detected immediately.

The 184-inch magnet
with Paul Aebersold
in the gap.
Berkeley, January 14,
1942.
*Photographer: D.
Cooksey.
Courtesy of Lawrence
Berkeley Laboratory*

The 184-inch
cyclotron building
above the University
of California Berkeley
campus. November 20,
1941.
*Photographer: D.
Cooksey.
Courtesy of Lawrence
Berkeley Laboratory*

E.O. Lawrence was the director of the Radiation Laboratory at Berkeley, California, and the inventor of the cyclotron, a device which smashed atomic nuclei with highly accelerated particles. In late 1941, Lawrence built a new cyclotron, with an immensely powerful 184-inch magnet. He later convinced General Groves to use the cyclotron as the basis for the electromagnetic separation of uranium isotopes at Oak Ridge.

The mass spectrometer was the principle tool of electromagnetic separation. Lawrence designed an apparatus he named a calutron which used the cyclotron as a mass spectrometer to separate isotopes according to weight. A receiver caught the stream of rare uranium-235 isotopes at the end of the process. In 1943, the Stone & Webster Engineering Company built the electromagnetic plant at Oak Ridge, code-named Y-12; it was operated by Tennessee Eastman, a subsidiary of Eastman Kodak.

The Y-12 plant consisted of an Alpha and a Beta building, where the enrichment took place in two stages. Each housed modified calutrons, called racetracks. Research, design, and construction proceeded simultaneously, as there was no time to build a pilot. The final plant, which cost 427 million dollars to complete, consisted of 500 racetracks, 268 buildings, and employed a peak operating force of 24,000 people.

Y-12's Alpha building
under construction.
Oak Ridge, June 1943.
Photographer: E.
Westcott.
Courtesy of NARA

Racetrack under construction.
Oak Ridge, 1943
Photographer: E. Westcott.
Courtesy of NARA

Completed racetrack.
Oak Ridge, 1944.
Photographer: E. Westcott.
Courtesy of NARA

The first operational weeks of the Y-12 plant Alpha stage were not auspicious. Problems developed when flawed magnetic coils caused shorts and variances in the magnetic fields. The entire factory had to be shut down for several weeks while the electromagnets were sent back to Allis-Chalmers (the Milwaukee factory that had built them), where they were cleaned and rewound.

The Allis-Chalmers factory floor where the electromagnets were produced. Milwaukee, 1943.

Photographer: Unknown. Courtesy of the Milwaukee County Historical Society

So little copper was available during the war that Groves borrowed 400 million dollars worth of silver (395 million troy ounces) from the U.S. Treasury to make the electromagnetic coil windings.

Y-12 "gunk" extraction
towers.
Oak Ridge, 1944.
Photographer: E. Westcott.
Courtesy of NARA

It was imperative to
recover every trace of
the valuable uranium-
235 from the calutron
receivers. In order to
accomplish this, the

Beta chemistry
facilities included
batteries of extractors,
filters, centrifuges,
evaporators, and
driers.

Completed building
9212 at Y-12.
Oak Ridge,
December 1945.

Photographer: E. Westcott.
Courtesy of NARA

**Uranium-235 was so
valuable that the
buildings housing the
higher quality stages
of the enrichment
process were heavily**

**guarded, even within
the military enclave of
Oak Ridge.**

S-50 Process columns under construction. Oak Ridge, 1945.
Photographer: E. Westcott. Courtesy of NARA

Thermal diffusion, or S-50, as it was code-named, was the last separation method to be implemented at Oak Ridge. Early research on it had been done by the navy, but the army considered the Manhattan Project its own territory — and anyway, Groves felt this was an impractical method for use on an industrial scale. By 1943, however, the general realized that the amount of uranium being enriched in K-25 and Y-12 was not sufficient and so, in 1944, on the recommendation of Robert Oppenheimer, this third process was reconsidered.

Thermal diffusion worked by moving uranium hexafluoride gas through columns forty-eight feet high. Each column consisted of three pipes — nickel, copper, and iron — placed one within another. The nickel pipe was heated with steam, so that the lighter isotopes collected near the warm wall, while the heavier isotopes gravitated toward the water-cooled copper pipe.

Cubicle operators
at Y-12.
Oak Ridge, 1944.
Photographer: E. Westcott.
Courtesy of NARA

Thousands of opera-
tors were employed at
the Y-12 plant; most
were women. As was
true of all the other
workers at Oak Ridge

and Hanford, they
never knew the real
purpose or character
of the product they
were making until
after the war.

Opposite:

Post-war public relations photograph in front of X-10. Oak Ridge, c. 1945–46.
Photographer: E. Westcott. Courtesy of NARA

A local Girl Scout troop was photographed outside the experimental nuclear reactor X-10, after Hiroshima, in a public-relations gesture to show that no dangers existed within the "atomic city."

MAKING THE BOMB BY HAND

"A LITTLE BOMB LIKE THAT," ENRICO FERMI SAID IN 1939, LOOKING OUT OF HIS COLUMBIA OFFICE WINDOW, "AND IT WOULD ALL DISAPPEAR." — *The Physicists,* by Daniel J. Kevles

HAHN AND STRASSMAN'S 1938 discovery of fission meant that an atomic bomb could theoretically be made. In the United States, it was the fear that Hitler's Germany might be the first to make, and use, an atomic bomb that initially drove several physicists to enlist the support of the American government. In so doing, they inexorably bound science to the military. Three émigré physicists — Leo Szilard, Eugene Wigner, and Edward Teller — visited another transplanted European, Albert Einstein, and urged him to write directly to the American President. They wanted to impress upon President Roosevelt and the American military establishment that an entirely new weapon, using uranium and possessing the potential for immense destruction, was on the horizon, and that the Germans had suddenly halted all exports of the metal. It took two years and the shock of Pearl Harbor to galvanize the American government into formally organizing an atomic bomb project, but in the meantime Szilard did receive $6,000 from the United States government. He used the small sum to pursue a vision of nearly a decade's duration — the demonstration of a self-sustaining nuclear chain reaction.

The Manhattan Project was launched in August 1942; and on December 2, 1942, a team led by Enrico Fermi, with Leo Szilard, produced the first artificial, self-sustaining nuclear chain reaction at the University of Chicago. The pile of graphite and uranium, which was laboriously laid by hand over several weeks, demonstrated that the release of energy stored in heavy nuclei could be sustained. The atomic bomb was now more than just an idea on a blackboard.

The Manhattan Engineering District came to comprise over thirty different research and production sites; many were located in universities and colleges across the United States. Eventually, research was consolidated at Site Y, Los Alamos, which had the task of preparing a practical military weapon for use as soon as sufficient fissionable material became available. When Leo Szilard heard about the isolated location he quipped, "Nobody could think straight in a place like that. Everybody who goes there will go crazy." (Tensions between Szilard and General Groves prevented Szilard from ever visiting the mesa to find out.)

Theoretical physicist Robert Oppenheimer was selected by Groves to direct the laboratory. Many of the scientists traveled to New Mexico not knowing just what they would be working on or how they would live. Arriving at a small railway station in Lamy, New Mexico, their next stop was at an office in Santa Fe, before they were driven up the treacherous road to Los Alamos. Most worked within groups of about a dozen people, each headed by a group leader directly responsible to Oppenheimer. The divisions included: theoretical, experimental, ordnance, engineering, chemistry and metallurgy, explosives, and research. Early on, the scientists adopted the nickname "gadget" for the bomb that would dominate all of their lives for the duration of the Project and, for some, through many years to come.

The Chicago pile was the world's first nuclear reactor, but an atomic bomb was another matter entirely. A conventional explosive, such as dynamite, can be detonated at any time in any amount. In an atomic explosion, however, a critical mass is required: if a sufficient amount is assembled it will blow itself apart with enormous energy release — and if not, the material will just sit there, like copper or iron. The physicists had to answer crucial questions about materials of which little was known: what was the exact amount of material needed? How could a critical mass be assembled? Could it be detonated at a precise moment? And, finally, how could the assembled materials be kept together long enough for a vast explosion to occur?

These questions kept the Los Alamos scientists working long days during the laboratory's twenty-eight demanding months. In addition, the work required mathematicians and technicians, hand calculations, and workshop skills.

An intensive research project such as that at Los Alamos could, as Eugene Wigner once remarked to Fermi, have all the money it needed and more, but its success also hinged on a driving purpose and an inspirational leader. Although other physicists were capable of handling the scientific aspects of the project, none but Robert Oppenheimer possessed the combination of acute intelligence, scientific knowledge, human sensitivity, and drive that was vital for Los Alamos to thrive. He understood that it would be impossible to move ahead with sufficient speed if his fellow scientists could not work as a freely communicating team. He argued with Groves and won his point: unlike every other area of the Manhattan District, there was no compartmentalization at the laboratory. Oppenheimer could hire whomever he wished, and he quickly built a reputation as an efficient administrator.

The first atomic bombs were made by extremely young people, and the technical and moral territory they explored was new. For some of the scientists, the initial reasons for working on the bomb were compelling, but its effects left them deeply disturbed. After the war, Oppenheimer bade farewell to his former colleagues, some of whom had vowed to abandon weapons work after Hiroshima, saying, "But when you come right down to it the reason that we did this job is because it was an organic necessity. If you are a scientist you cannot stop such a thing. If you are a scientist you believe that it is good to find out how the world works; that it is good to find out what the realities are; that it is good to turn over to mankind at large the greatest possible power to control the world and to deal

with it according to its lights and its values." It was a consoling argument for many of the conflicted scientists who were nevertheless painfully aware that the power they had unleashed entailed an unprecedented political and moral responsibility that they, and the rest of humankind, now had to bear.

Enrico Fermi.
Los Alamos, c. 1944.
Photographer: Unknown.
Courtesy of Nella Fermi
Weiner

Opposite:

Uranium metal cubes.
Los Alamos, 1945.

Photographer: Unknown.
Courtesy of LANL

The world's first controlled nuclear chain reaction was initiated by Enrico Fermi, after a pause for lunch, on Wednesday, December 2, 1942. CP-1 was the world's first nuclear reactor and was referred to as a "pile" by those who constructed it. After Fermi had conducted his dramatic demonstration, officials in Washington, D.C., were told by telephone, "The Italian navigator has landed in the new world."

In the preparation for making the chain-reacting pile self-sustaining, sixteen smaller pile experiments were performed to determine the exact configuration of uranium within a graphite lattice. The uranium oxide was pressed into shapes called "pseudo-spheres." Each piece of graphite was individually machined, and produced a black dust. "We breathed it, slipped on it, and it oozed out of our pores," Al Wattenberg remembered.

An exponential pile at the University of Chicago. September–November 1945.
Photographer: Unknown. Courtesy of Argonne National Laboratory

The first three layers of graphite for CP-1 stacked on the floor of a squash court under the west stands of the Stagg Field Stadium at the University of Chicago, November 1942.

Photographer: Unknown. Courtesy of Argonne National Laboratory

The graphite and uranium were piled in a roughly spherical shape, supported by a wooden frame. Into it were slotted several wooden rods covered in cadmium. The subtlety of the mechanism was not visible: when the control rods were pulled out, more atoms of uranium-235 flew apart, up to a trillion each second, as a neutron hit; each time releasing two or more neutrons per fission. The neutrons slowed down after many bounces off the graphite, and their potential capture by the uranium-238 atoms, which were not chain reacting, was prevented by the presence of uranium as lumps in the lattice. The slowed neutrons then caused fission in uranium-235 atoms, liberating an additional generation of neutrons. One half watt of power was produced for four-and-a-half minutes before Fermi shut down the pile. It was the first energy released by humans on earth that had not originated from the sun.

Fermi's colleague, Eugene Wigner, who had brought a bottle of Chianti, recalled "Nothing very spectacular happened. Nothing had moved and the pile itself had given no sound. Nevertheless, when the rods were pushed back in and the clicking died down, we suddenly experienced a let-down feeling, for all of us understood the language of the counter. Even though we had anticipated the success of the experiment, its accomplishment had a deep impact on us. For some time we had known that we were about to unlock a giant; still we could not escape an eerie feeling when we knew we had actually done it. We felt as, I presume, everyone feels who has done something that he knows will have very far-reaching consequences which he cannot foresee."

Layers 27, 28, and 29
of CP-1.
University of Chicago,
November 24, 1942.
Photographer: Unknown.
Courtesy of Argonne
National Laboratory

The curtain in the
back is a huge square
rubber balloon that
had been specifically
made by Goodyear in
case the pile needed to
be operated in a
vacuum: too many
neutrons might be
absorbed by the
nitrogen in the air if
there was insufficient
uranium inside the
pile. Graphite of
extremely high purity
had also been manu-
factured to reduce the
absorption of neu-
trons.

J. Robert
Oppenheimer's I.D.
badge photograph.
Los Alamos, 1943.
Photographer: Unknown.
Courtesy of LANL

J. R. Oppenheimer

The West Gate
entrance to Los
Alamos, c. 1943.
Photographer: Unknown.
Courtesy of LANL

The Chicago reactor demonstrated a chain reaction, but it could not explode like an atomic bomb because it depended on the rather gradual slowing down of neutrons by collision with the graphite. Several months later, the task at Los Alamos was to produce a violent and explosive chain reaction that would involve a very different arrangement of fissionable materials.

The laboratory in New Mexico was established to bring together the keenest scientific minds and hands in the United States. In a matter of months, the greatest ad-hoc physics department in the world coalesced at Los Alamos. Laboratory director Oppenheimer understood that the intensive effort necessary to design and make an atomic bomb required that all key personnel be located together. Referring to Los Alamos, one historian has said, "More scientific brainpower was accumulated there than at any time since Isaac Newton dined alone," but General Groves thought otherwise. He was once heard to remark, "At great expense we gathered on this mesa the largest collection of crackpots ever seen."

The laboratory's real purpose was a tightly-guarded secret. Oppenheimer suggested that curious locals be told that rockets were being made. He sent several army officers and scientists to Santa Fe to repeat similar stories, but the efforts usually met with little success. Sometimes other, more fantastic rumors were circulated — that Los Alamos was a maternity home for WACS, for instance, or that it manufactured submarine windshield wipers.

Left, from top:

Herbert Bridge photographing the Cyclotron Group, led by Robert Wilson. Los Alamos, 1944.
Photographer: Herbert Bridge.
Courtesy of Robert R. Wilson

The Cyclotron Group. Los Alamos, 1944.
Photographer: Herbert Bridge.
Courtesy of Robert R. Wilson

Discussion on the terrace of Fuller Lodge at a Nuclear Physics Conference. Los Alamos, 1946. From left to right: Bob Davis, Nick Metropolis, Stan Ulam, Ed McMillan, and Freddy de Hoffman.
Photographer: J.J. Mike Michnovicz.
Courtesy of the Ulam Collection

Right:
The Radioactivity Group, led by Emilio Segrè, photographed outside the Technical Area. Los Alamos, 1945.
Photographer: Jack Aeby.
Courtesy of Jack Aeby

The scientific community at Los Alamos was unique. Weekly colloquia were open to scientists in all groups and divisions. Informal discussions at lunch, in the labs, and on hikes were as important to the work at hand as formal research methods. "Everyone," wrote Bernice Brode, "wore casual clothes, jeans or old unpressed pants, open shirts and no ties and I don't recall seeing a shined pair of shoes during working hours. They all seemed to be enjoying themselves, as scientists always do when they ponder their problems together."

These scientists also soberly discussed the possibility that Germany might have initiated an atomic bomb program of its own. Werner Heisenberg, one of the world's foremost nuclear

Group and Division leaders outside the Technical Area. Los Alamos, c. 1944. From left to right: Herb Anderson, Darol Froman, Enrico Fermi, Heinz Barschall, Robert Wilson, Hans Bethe, John Manley, Seth Neddermeyer, L.D.P. King, George Kistiakowsky, Emilio Segrè, and Robert Bacher.
Photographer: Jack Aeby.
Courtesy of Jack Aeby

K. E. J. Fuchs

Above:
Jack Clark, Enrico Fermi, Carson Mark, and Richard Feynman having lunch at Fuller Lodge. Los Alamos, 1944.
Photographer: Unknown.
Courtesy of Nella Fermi Weiner

physicists and a colleague of many at Los Alamos, had, during Hitler's rise to power, declined numerous teaching posts in the United States. His mentor and friend Niels Bohr was convinced Heisenberg was working on the bomb for Germany. Many of the other European-born scientists felt similarly about their German counterparts. Eugene Wigner refused to let General Groves fingerprint him for security purposes: "A fingerprint record might someday fall into the hands of the Nazis. I had no doubt that if the Germans won the war they would swiftly begin rounding up everyone in the Manhattan Project for execution. And the roundup would go easier with fingerprints."

Klaus Fuchs's I.D. badge photograph. Los Alamos, 1944.
Photographer: Unknown. Courtesy of LANL

Klaus Fuchs had come to Los Alamos with the British Mission. He was a valued member of the Theoretical Division, according to physicist John Manley, who remembered,

"He worked very hard; worked very hard for us, for this country. His trouble was that he worked very hard for Russia too." Fuchs's name would later appear with others from Los Alamos on one of the basic patents for the hydrogen bomb in the United States.

The Technical Area consisted of several pre-fabricated buildings near Ashley Pond, surrounded by a fence. According to Charlotte Serber, they had "a cluttered, disorderly, academic air. The offices were simple enough, though incredibly dirty, over-crowded, and badly equipped." As research progressed, more structures were erected in the surrounding canyons and mesas, prompting Bernice Brode to comment, "We complained that the Technical Area was expanding in all directions into ancient unspoiled land, and installations grew up in place of wind-fashioned pines and shrubs and colored rocks. Quonset huts were shamelessly erected in front of cliff dwellings, manned with soldiers with guns . . ."

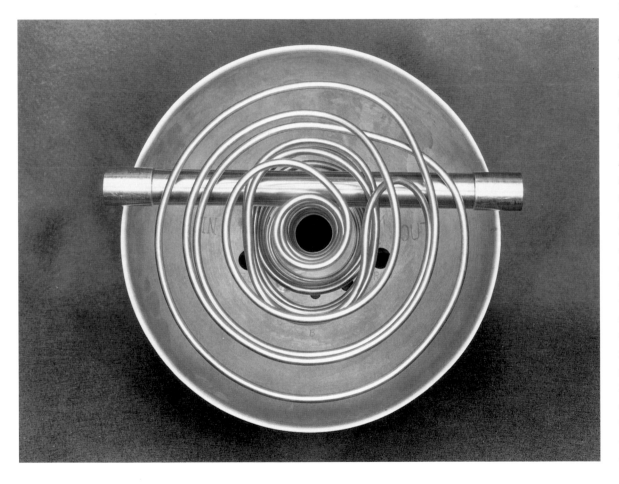

One of the earliest experiments used almost pure uranium-235 to determine the critical mass necessary for a self-sustaining nuclear chain reaction. A hollow stainless steel sphere, one foot in diameter, and surrounded by a beryllium oxide reflector, contained a solution of water and uranyl sulphate. The solution was made up from the first small delivery of uranium-235 received from Oak Ridge. The first device was called LOPO (for low power) and ran at 30 milliwatts. Later versions of this device such as SUPO contained cooling coils to permit operation up to 30 kilowatts to provide a strong neutron source. Though these devices were unlike the metallic bomb core (depending on slow neutrons), they provided the first means by which researchers could validate their theories for calculating critical masses, and also provided a means for determining the neutron properties of many elements. The devices were code-named the "Water Boiler," and the experiments continued throughout the war and beyond.

There was not enough plutonium-239 or uranium-235 to make a bomb in 1943. No one knew exactly how much would be necessary to make an explosive chain reaction (called a supercritical mass). One major challenge at Los Alamos was to design the bomb and devise a manufacturing method before the essential fuel had been produced. Critical assembly experiments used sub-critical and critical mass amounts of the fissionable material, once they became available from Oak Ridge and Hanford, to check the predicted calculations for the supercritical mass. These experiments measured how many neutrons were being created and lost, and how the process was affected by the shape, density, and purity of the fissionable material used. The experiments were crucial, since it was neutrons that liberated the energy stored in matter.

An experiment to determine the fast-neutron critical mass of uranium-235 in metal form. As more uranium-235 became available, bars of uranium hydride were stacked in a subcritical mass, surrounded by tamper blocks of beryllium to reflect neutrons back into the uranium mass. **Los Alamos, c. 1944.** *Photographer: Unknown. Courtesy of LANL*

A disassembled film badge, designed to monitor an individual's exposure to radioactivity. The unexposed piece of film would fog in relation to the levels of radioactivity present. Los Alamos, c. 1944.

Photographer: Unknown.
Courtesy of NARA

Two different means of achieving a supercritical mass of uranium or plutonium were explored at Los Alamos. The gun-assembly method was based on existing "smokeless powder" gun techniques: half the critical amount of uranium-235 was placed as a target at one end of a gun and the other half shot as a projectile at the target. Within a few thousandths of a second after firing, the supercritical mass was achieved. The implosion method was based on the concept of using high explosives wrapped around the fissionable material. When the high explosives were detonated, the solid metal was compressed into a supercritical mass. The gun-assembly method had initially been selected to trigger both the uranium and plutonium gadgets, but a crisis occurred in the spring of 1944 with the discovery that large numbers of neutrons were liberated by the spontaneous fission of plutonium. The gun's assembly time would thus be much too slow to compress a supercritical mass of plutonium, thus reducing the explosive yield. Because the Manhattan Engineering District had already committed so much time, money, and effort to making plutonium, another design had to be invented. The entire laboratory was reorganized in August of 1944 to accomplish this single goal, leaving only Robert Serber and his small group to complete the uranium gadget.

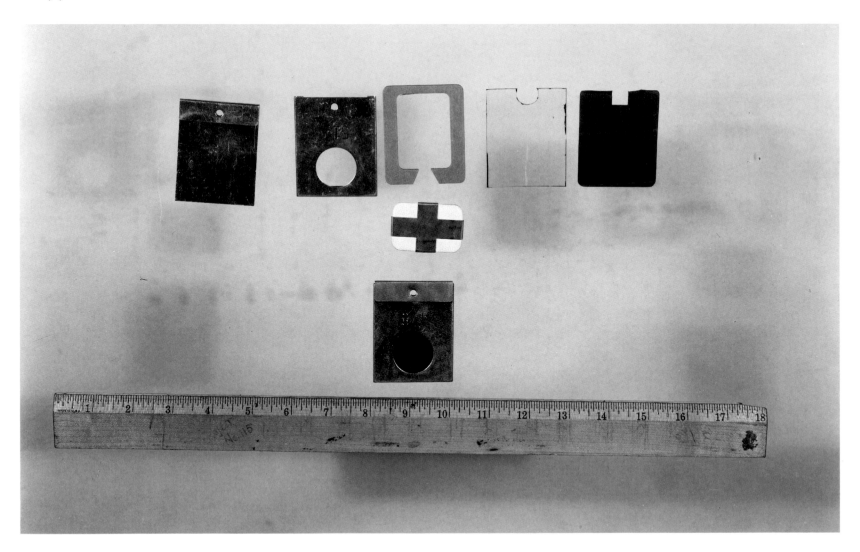

Strict rules were instituted when handling critical assemblies: no one was to work alone, nor handle a piece of material that, if dropped, could cause an assembly to become critical. However, there was a certain bravado among the physicists: some felt "impervious to the invisible danger" of the work, according to Otto Frisch. After the war, Harry Daghlian was working by himself at night on August 21, 1945 in the Omega laboratory on this critical assembly. A tamper brick slipped from his hand. According to the accident report, he "instinctively and immediately pushed this brick off the assembly with his right hand." The brilliant blue glow of ionized air he observed around the assembly indicated an acute dose of radiation. The assembly had reached supercriticality but did not explode because the mass of plutonium immediately expanded and halted the run-away chain reaction. The effects of radiation on his living tissue were the same as if a bomb had exploded. Daghlian permitted himself to be photographed until his death twenty-five days later, at 4:30 PM, Saturday, September 15, 1945.

A critical assembly with plutonium. The plutonium sphere is surrounded by tamper blocks. Omega laboratory. Los Alamos, August 1945.
Photographer: Unknown.
Courtesy of LANL

Opposite:

**Harry Daghlian's
hand, severely burned
by fast neutrons and
gamma rays.
Los Alamos Hospital,
September 1945.**

*Photographer: J.J. Mike
Michnovicz.*

Courtesy of LANL

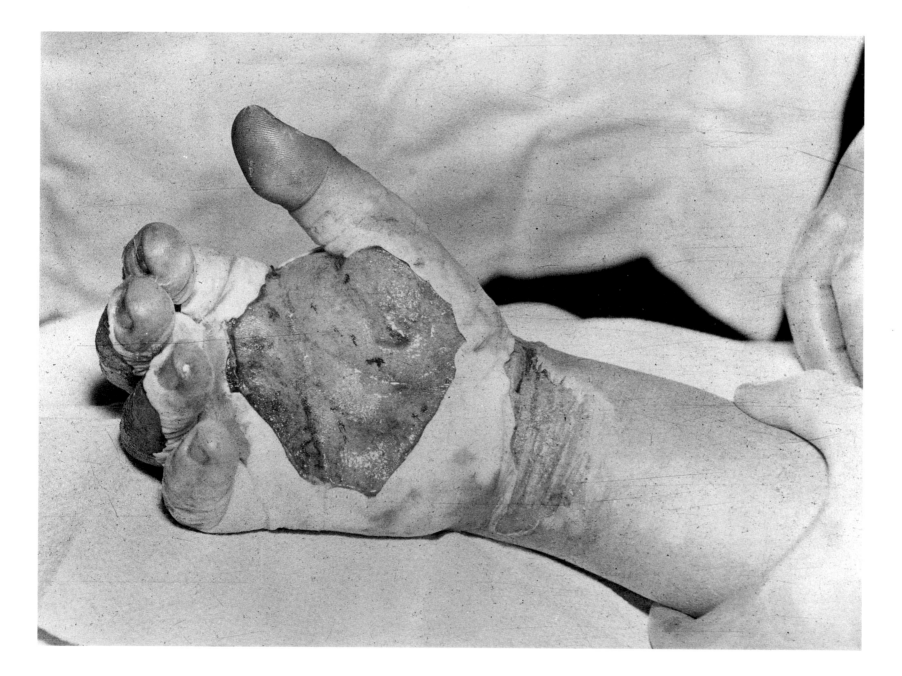

Radiation safety was a serious problem for the Manhattan District. The organized monitoring of personnel and establishment of safe radiation levels were handled by a newly-formed "health physics" division. Among their concerns were the development of instrumentation and of tolerance standards, research into the short-term and long-term effects of radioactivity, and radioactive waste disposal.

Since so little was known about the effects of radiation, animal studies were conducted. When plutonium manufacture began, several members of the Health Group thought it necessary to learn more about its potential effects. In 1945, while scientists were handling plutonium, and the danger of overexposure was constant, some worried that the existing protection was insufficient. Oppenheimer wrote to the Chief Medical Officer: "We all have the feeling that at the present time the hazards of workers at Site Y are probably very much more serious than those at any other branch of the Project . . ." Also, at this time, discussions began within the laboratory about implementing human studies experiments with plutonium. These experiments were eventually conducted at the Universities of Rochester and California at Berkeley, among other MED official research sites.

A 1946 reconstruction of the second fatal criticality accident, which occurred after the war.

Los Alamos, May 21, 1946. *Photographer: Unknown. Courtesy of LANL*

Louis Slotin, leader of the Critical Assemblies Group at the time, was demonstrating criticality measurements for the upcoming Bikini tests by separating two plutonium/beryllium hemispheres with a screwdriver and then gradually permitting them to get closer, when the screwdriver accidentally slipped. All eight scientists in the room received large doses of radiation, but Slotin's was acute. He died nine days later. All critical assembly experiments performed by hand were forbidden after this accident.

An early experiment for detonating the implosion gadget. Los Alamos, 1944. *Photographer: Unknown. Courtesy of LANL*

Synchronized electric detonators had to be designed so that each piece of high explosive wrapped around the plutonium would explode simultaneously. Each detonator fired a special high explosive "lens," launching a collapsing spherical detonation wave intended to compress the fissile metal core. The detonators also had to be made rugged and reliable enough to withstand a high altitude flight.

CLASSIFICATION CANCELLED
PER DOC REVIEW JAN. 1973

An implosion test at Anchor Ranch, or S-site, where hundreds of test implosions were seen and heard by the residents. Los Alamos, c. 1944. *Photographer: Unknown. Courtesy of LANL*

Below: An early implosion experiment. TNT was wrapped around a hollow steel cylinder (the center ring) in an attempt to squash the steel pipes into a solid bar. Los Alamos, c. 1943. *Photographer: Unknown. Courtesy of LANL*

The idea of implosion had first been suggested at a Berkeley physics conference in 1942. At Los Alamos, implosion research was later taken over by George Kistiakowsky, a Russian-born chemist and explosives expert. He and his colleagues swung between optimism and pessimism. Kistiakowsky wrote his own comic analysis of the months to come: "During October . . . it is hoped, [the implosion staff] will be in a position to recommend a design of the gadget which will have a finite chance of properly functioning . . . [For] November and December, the test gadget failed. Project staff resumes frantic work. Kistiakowsky goes nuts and is locked up." Because the implosion device was such a complex enterprise and its viability uncertain, the largest experiment of the Manhattan Project (code-named Trinity) was planned for the summer of 1945. It would be a full-scale test of a plutonium bomb.

A dummy unit to
house the implosion
gadget.
Wendover Field, Utah,
1945.
Photographer: Unknown.
Courtesy of LANL

While the design of the two bomb mechanisms was being completed, the means of dropping them was discussed. Project A (Alberta) was responsible for the combat use of the first atomic bombs. Los Alamos physicist and U.S. Navy Captain W.S. Parsons was commander of the project, which had three objectives: designing the two bombs' ballistic shapes, training the flight crews to drop them, and preparing an overseas base for their delivery. Project A would also handle the final assembly of the bombs prior to releasing them. At Los Alamos, ballistics, fusing, detonation, and aircraft release mechanisms were handled. At Wendover, Utah, crews began to train in the spring of 1945 for their upcoming missions. From October 1944 until August 1945, 155 dummy units were dropped in the United States alone.

As the Manhattan Project moved ahead with the preparation and fueling of the bombs in the spring of 1945, General Groves authorized an intelligence mission, code-named Alsos (meaning "grove" in Greek), to travel to Europe. This team, made up of Manhattan Project physicists and intelligence officers, was to gather information about nuclear activities in Europe. The Alsos team only uncovered "a little underground cave, a wing of a small textile factory (and) a few rooms in an old brewery," according to Dutch-born physicist Samuel Goudsmit. Alsos also located some important scientific documents, seized nuclear materials, including a large amount of high-quality uranium ore, and captured the most talented German scientists — including Werner Heisenberg and Otto Hahn.

Discovery of uranium fuel pellets buried in a field.
Alsos mission.
Germany, April 1945.
Photographer: D. Collins.
Courtesy of R. Kathren

Below:
Bottom section of Heisenberg's dismantled reactor. He had not yet demonstrated a self-sustaining nuclear chain reaction with his "uranium machine" by 1945.
Alsos mission.
Haigerloch, Germany, April 1945.
Photographer: D. Collins.
Courtesy of R. Kathren

Opposite:

**Plutonium metal
buttons.
Los Alamos, 1945.**
*Photographer: Unknown.
Courtesy of LANL*

The last day of the pre-nuclear age. The plutonium bomb sat on a 100-foot tower, waiting for dawn.

Thunderstorms gathered in the Jornada del Muerto, dangerously close to the tower. July 15, 1945.

Photographer: L.D.P. King.
Courtesy of L.D.P. King

TRINITY

MY REAWAKENING FROM BEING COMPLETELY TECHNICALLY ORIENTED CAME DRAMATICALLY ON JULY 16 AS I EXPERIENCED THE TEST EXPLOSION OF THE FIRST NUCLEAR BOMB . . . THAT WHICH HAD BEEN AN INTELLECTUAL REALITY TO ME FOR SOME THREE YEARS HAD SUDDENLY BECOME A FACTUAL, AN EXISTENTIAL REALITY. THERE IS A VERY GREAT DIFFERENCE. — *The Conscience of a Physicist,* by Robert R. Wilson

THE MOST CRUCIAL experiment of the Manhattan Project was the test of the plutonium bomb at Trinity, near Alamogordo, New Mexico, on July 16, 1945. The scientists were confident early on that the uranium gun-assembly bomb would work, but the implosion device, translated by the physicists, chemists, and engineers at Site Y in a few short months from theory into a practical bomb design, was riddled with unknowns. Planning for a test therefore began in December 1944, when small amounts of plutonium arrived on the Los Alamos mesa from Berkeley. Physicist Kenneth T. Bainbridge was selected as the test's director, and it was he who led the search for a suitable stretch of land for the experiment. Eight sites in four states were considered, but ultimately a desert valley which lay between the Rio Grande river and the Sierra Oscura mountains in New Mexico, known as the Jornada del Muerto, was chosen. Oppenheimer gave the test its code-name: Trinity.

During the spring of 1945, when work for the test grew feverish, two external events shook the nation and the Manhattan Project: one was the death of President Roosevelt in April; the other was Germany's surrender a month later. Some of the scientists now harbored doubts about the need to use the bomb, despite the ongoing war with Japan.

However, most of the scientists were too absorbed by the technical question of whether or not the bomb would work to philosophize. They traveled the hard roads between Los Alamos, Albuquerque, and Socorro, in large convoys of trucks and equipment. An improvised base camp was strewn with miles of wire and thousands of pieces of sensitive instrumentation. A dress rehearsal shot was organized in May, using 100 tons of TNT. The shot, a pale version of what was to come, enabled the scientists to recalibrate instrumentation and to exert pressure upon the military to give serious thought to the potential effects of radioactive fallout.

Groves had agreed to schedule the Trinity test so that President Truman could learn its result by the time of his meeting at Potsdam with Stalin and Churchill. As the sixteenth of July approached, the plutonium core was driven on a bumpy road in an army jeep to the Trinity site, where it was unloaded and assembled in the living room of a vacated ranch.

Thunderstorms caused the test to be postponed for several hours. Some who glimpsed a pacing, chain-smoking Oppenheimer were worried that he was near collapse. Others played poker. The physicists took bets on the explosion's yield. Fermi infuriated Groves and Bainbridge by speculating aloud whether the explosion might ignite the atmosphere. When the bomb finally exploded at dawn, after a tense countdown, Fermi could be seen throwing bits of paper into the air to measure the blast. This primitive calculation method proved to be almost as accurate as all the modern equipment spread across the desert sand. So preoccupied was Fermi with his experiment that he claimed never to have heard the huge sound which accompanied the first man-made atomic explosion. It was a sound none of his colleagues would ever forget.

Julian Mack, head of
the Optics Group,
surveying bunker sites
at zero: the point over
which the implosion
device would be
detonated.
March 19, 1945.
Photographer:
E. Wallace?
Courtesy of LANL

Base camp, Trinity,
lay eleven miles south
of zero.
April 1945.

Photographer:
E. Wallace?
Courtesy of LANL

So little plutonium had been manufactured in 1944 that Groves worried about the possibility that, should the explosion fail, he would be held accountable for millions of dollars worth of lost plutonium. A massive steel vessel to contain the explosion was therefore ordered. Even before it was built, the container was nicknamed Jumbo.

Jumbo arrived at an abandoned railway siding at Pope, New Mexico, April 13, 1945.
Photographer: E. Wallace?
Courtesy of LANL

Jumbo posed problems from the start. Many scaled-down designs, dubbed Jumbinos, were tested. It was difficult to find a company willing to construct the massive container, or to arrange transportation. A flat car was especially adapted to carry the heaviest object ever transported by rail.

Jumbo weighed 214 tons and was 25 feet long and 12 feet wide. Its walls were 14 inches thick. May 1945.
Photographer: E. Wallace? Courtesy of LANL

Caterpillar trailers dragged the steel object across the desert. May 1945.
Photographer: E. Wallace? Courtesy of LANL

Jumbo was lowered into the base of its specially constructed tower.
May 1945.
Photographer:
E. Wallace?
Courtesy of LANL

By the time Jumbo arrived at Trinity, confidence in the implosion design and in the production of plutonium had both increased. Since the vessel was now unnecessary, the scientists placed it 800 yards west of zero and left it to withstand the effects of the explosions.

A wooden platform was built twenty feet high to support the crates of TNT and to replicate the scale of the Trinity test.

April–May 1945.
Photographer:
E. Wallace?
Courtesy of LANL

None of the scientists knew precisely how an explosion greater than a few tons of TNT would behave, so a dress rehearsal for the Trinity test was organized. 100 tons of TNT was detonated and spiked with fission products from Hanford to approximate, at a low level, the radioactivity the plutonium bombs would produce.

Men stacking crates of TNT.
May 1945.
Photographer:
E. Wallace?
Courtesy of LANL

Unloading the high explosives crates.
May 1945.
Photographer:
E. Wallace?
Courtesy of LANL

Radioactive fallout was still a relatively unknown phenomena before Trinity. After the 100-ton test, Stafford Warren of the MED, Louis Hempelmann and James Nolan, senior members of the Health Group, finally persuaded the army to prepare for the evacuation of nearby farms if atmospheric conditions should require this.

A uranium slug irradiated for 100 days at Hanford was prepared for insertion into the TNT. May 5, 1945.
Photographer: E. Wallace? Courtesy of LANL

At 04:37:05 on May 7, 1945, the day Germany surrendered, the world's largest, controlled explosion was detonated. The flash was seen sixty miles away, a cloud rose 15,000 feet into the air, and a twenty-nine foot wide crater was formed.

Photographer:
E. Wallace?
Courtesy of LANL

Jumbo with the
plutonium bomb
tower in the distance.
May 1945.
Photographer:
E. Wallace?
Courtesy of LANL

Jumbo displayed little
alteration after the
TNT explosion.
May 1945.
Photographer:
E. Wallace?
Courtesy of LANL

Miles of wires connecting the bunkers, instruments, base camp, and point zero.
Photographer: E. Wallace? Courtesy of LANL

Emilio Segrè in front of a barrage balloon.
Photographer: Jack Aeby. Courtesy of the Los Alamos Historical Society

Interior of Wilson's bunker.
Photographer: Unknown. Courtesy of Robert R. Wilson

Robert Wilson outside his bunker at 10,000 yards north of zero.
Photographer: Unknown. Courtesy of Robert R. Wilson

Working conditions in the Jornada del Muerto were difficult and security was stringent. Everyone worked ten to eighteen hour days, sometimes longer. The Project had the highest procurement priorities in the nation, yet something as mundane as garden hose (to protect cables connecting sensitive instrumentation), was still undelivered two weeks prior to the test.

Clyde Wiegand outside an instrumentation shelter.
Photographer: Jack Aeby.
Courtesy of Jack Aeby

Morale was high at Trinity, though living conditions were rudimentary. Base camp was hit twice by stray bombs dropped by bombers making practice runs from the nearby Alamogordo Bombing Range. The heat was blistering; the desert populated by scorpions and rattlesnakes.

From top:

SEDs John Leppman (pictured) and Carl Crumb tended a seismograph and microbarometer outside of Trinity, in San Antonio, New Mexico. The army kept seismographic records of the blast in case of lawsuits.
Photographer: Carl Crumb.
Courtesy of Carl Crumb

Herb Anderson, Jack Clark, Darragh Nagle, and Nat Sugarman, members of the Radio Chemistry Group, outside the McDonald Ranch.
Photographer: L.D.P. King.
Courtesy of L.D.P. King

On April 12, 1945, the flag at Trinity was hung at half-mast to mourn the death of President Roosevelt. Two weeks later, President Truman received his first briefing about the atomic bomb.
Photographer: E. Wallace?
Courtesy of LANL

A photographic
bunker, 800 yards
north of zero.
Photographer:
E. Wallace?
Courtesy of LANL

A flash bomb to illu-
minate the underside
of the cloud formed by
the explosion.
Photographer: E. Wallace?
Courtesy of LANL

A search light to
follow the explosion's
debris in the air.
Photographer:
E. Wallace?
Courtesy of LANL

A mechanical
impulse gauge with
golfing graffiti.
Photographer:
E. Wallace?
Courtesy of LANL

By May 1945 the Trinity base camp was the scene of hectic activity. Instruments were installed across the desert to record and study
the explosion. Sets of experiments would measure blast, shock, and
damage; others would check the detonators and the implosion
method. Radiochemical experiments would measure the yield of
the bomb. The test would also be photographed in great detail.

The plutonium core arrived at the McDonald Ranch for assembly on July 12, 1945. Inside the ventilated field case were two small, but very heavy, plutonium hemispheres for which the army requested a receipt.

Photographer: E. Wallace? Courtesy of LANL

Instructions for the assembly of the plutonium plug included:

"Pick up GENTLY . . . "Plug hole with a CLEAN cloth . . . "Sphere will be left overnight, cap up, on a small dishpan."

The sphere of high explosives arrived July 13, and was carefully unloaded at the base of the 100 foot tower.

Photographer: E. Wallace?
Courtesy of LANL

TR-310

SED Herb Lehr
holding the assembled
bomb core inside the
McDonald Ranch.
Photographer: E. Wallace?
Courtesy of LANL

A tent was erected around the base of the tower during the final assembly, which required the plutonium plug to be inserted into the sphere of the high explosives.
Photographer: E. Wallace?
Courtesy of LANL

A still from a motion picture documentation of the final bomb assembly. Oppenheimer, weighing less than 100 pounds and worn out from stress and a bout of chicken pox, looks over from the left.
Photographer: Unknown
Courtesy of LANL

The world's first atomic bomb. Norris Bradbury stands with an SED man on top of the tower. The installed detonators cover the gadget's surface.
July 15, 1945
Photographer: E. Wallace?
Courtesy of LANL

Thunderstorms on the eve of the explosion delayed the test and added to the anxiety and tension permeating Trinity. Groves took out his frustration on Jack Hubbard, the army meteorologist who had previously advised against the date.

At 4:00 AM the arming party opened the circuits, checked connections, and began the final countdown. The project staff gathered outside control bunkers at 10,000 yards north and west. All were told to lie flat and face down, feet towards zero. Edward Teller remembered: "No one complied. We were determined to look the beast in the eye." Welder's glass and suntan lotion were passed around, though *New York Times* science reporter William Laurence found it ". . . an eerie sight to see a number of our highest-ranking scientists seriously rubbing sunburn lotion on their faces and hands in the pitch-blackness of the night, twenty miles away from the expected flash."

Views from the bomb's tower, north and south, across the Jornada del Muerto.
Photographer: E. Wallace?
Courtesy of LANL

Compaña Hill, located twenty miles northwest of zero, was the overlook point for invited observers. Richard Feynman remembered, "We were all just watching quietly . . . The man standing next to me (William Laurence) said, "What's that?" I said, "That was the bomb."

Photographer: E. Wallace?
Courtesy of LANL

TR-150

View from 10,000 yards north of zero. 05:29 hours Mountain
War Time. July 16, 1945.

This image encompasses the initial four seconds of the explosion
on a single sheet of film. A noiseless flash broke the darkness.
Photographer: J. Mack.
Courtesy of LANL

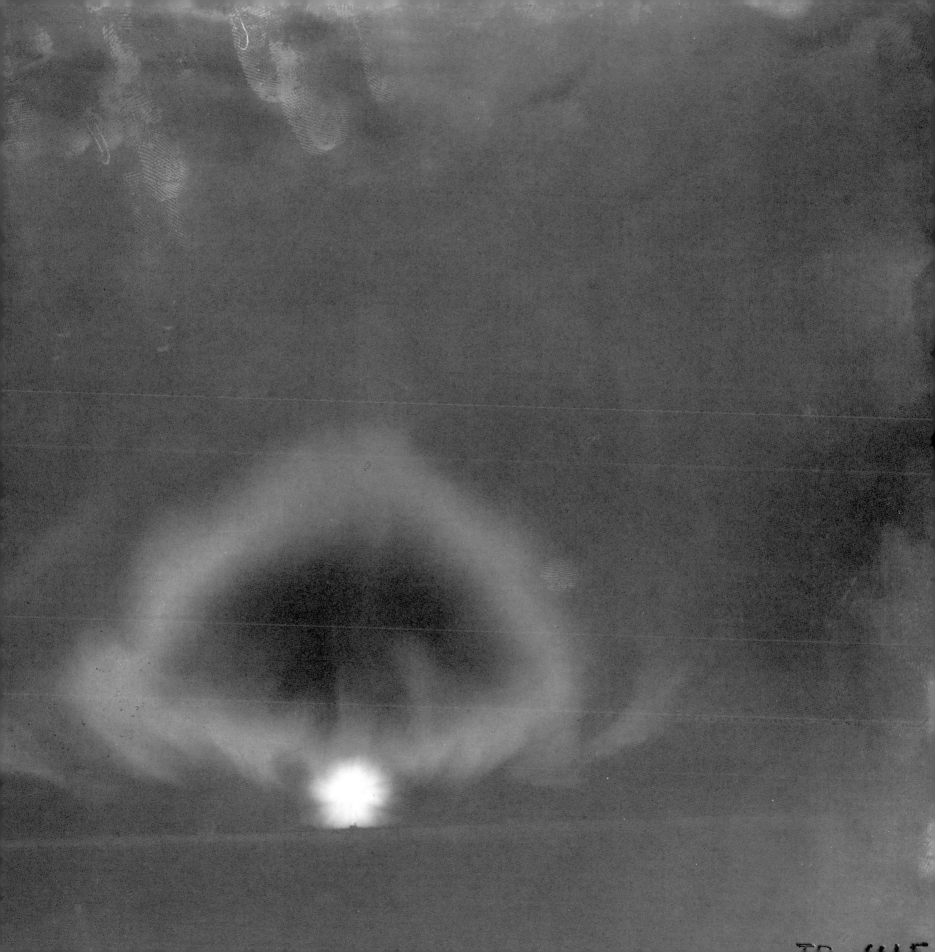

View from 800 yards west of zero. 0.10 milliseconds. (One thousandth of a second.) This is the earliest exposure of the nuclear age.

Photographer: B. Brixner.

Courtesy of LANL

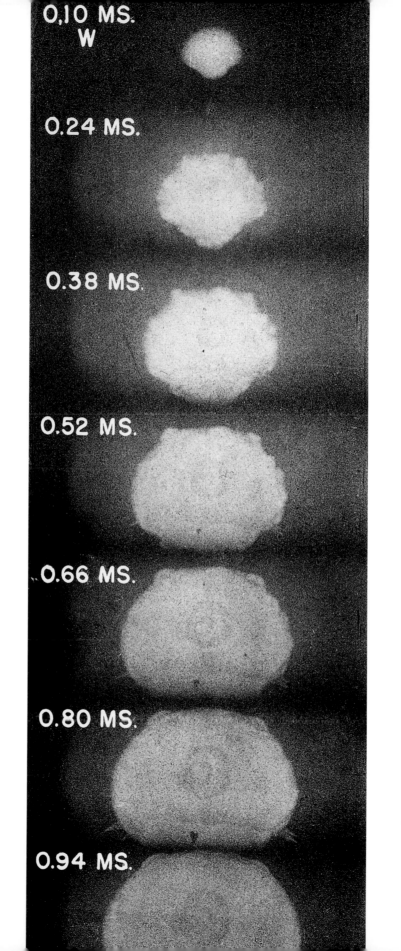

0,10 MS.
W

0.24 MS.

0.38 MS.

0.52 MS.

0.66 MS.

0.80 MS.

0.94 MS.

One hundred thousand photographic exposures were made of the explosion. None can convey the intensity of the blast, many times brighter than the sun and, for a fraction of a second, brighter than any light ever produced on earth. In several early exposures of the blast, the film is solarized and blistered by "what was perhaps the greatest photographic over-exposure ever made," according to Julian Mack. Most observers saw a very bright flash of light that illuminated the landscape. A ball of fire rose and expanded, still too bright to look at directly. The sky seemed to one observer to be "aglow with an orange hue," while others noticed a deep violet color due to the intense radioactivity permeating the air. Unexposed skin suddenly felt hot; anyone who tried to look even indirectly at the blast was temporarily blinded.

"The whole spectacle was so tremendous," Edwin McMillan later wrote, "and one might say fantastic that the immediate reaction of the watchers was one of awe rather than excitement. After some minutes of silence, a few people made remarks like, "Well, it worked."

Photographer: B. Brixner.
Courtesy of LANL

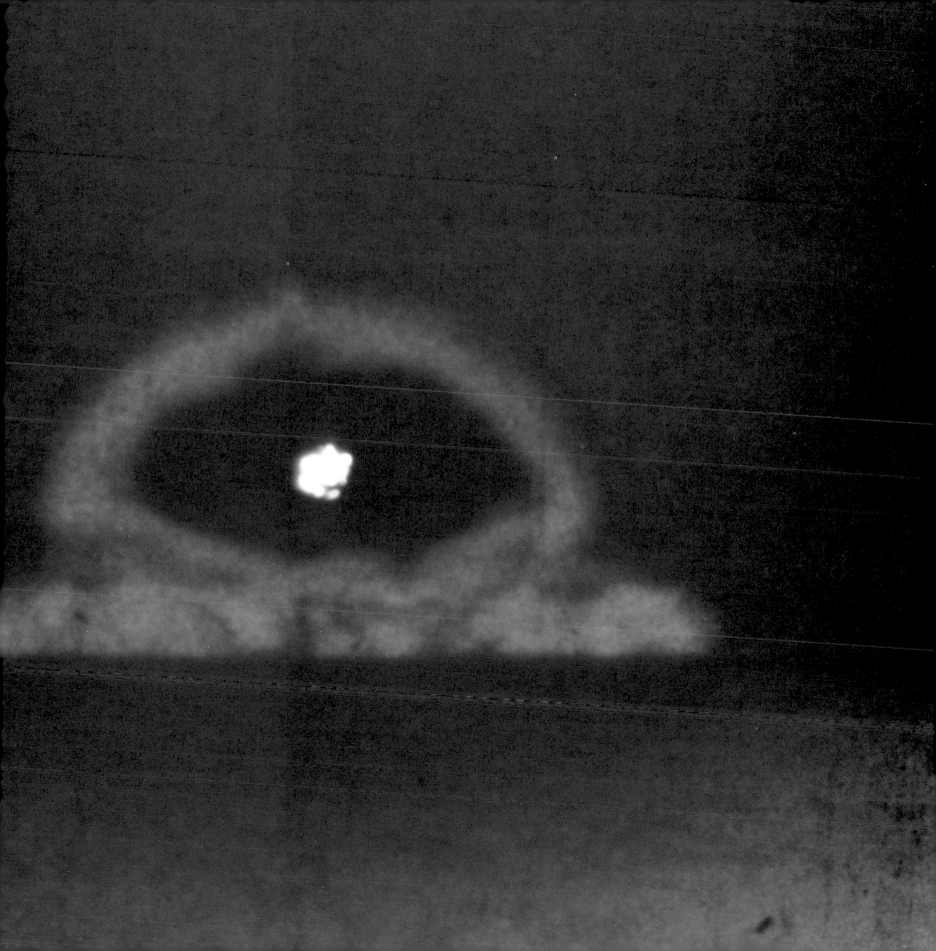

10,000 yards north.

At 6 milliseconds into the explosion, the fireball had struck the ground in the first exposure made by a Mitchell camera running at 120 frames per second (fps).

The ball of fire had no sharply defined boundaries. Instead, it was the shock front, so clearly defined in these images that was beginning to leave the ball of fire behind. The Mach wave — a bright belt — formed above the dust skirt. This is a reinforced shock wave caused by the explosion's heat reflecting off the ground as the fireball strikes. The Mach wave is stronger than the shock wave around the fireball.

On the right is a poorly exposed clock face Julian Mack had hoped to use to determine the exact timing of the fireball characteristics. There were more than forty-five cameras in operation inside four steel and concrete bunkers, at 800 and 10,000 yards north and west of zero. The fastest cameras, running over 7,100 fps were at the 800 yard stations but suffered the worst fogging. The 10,000 yard stations housed the motion picture cameras.

Photographer: B. Brixner.
Courtesy of LANL

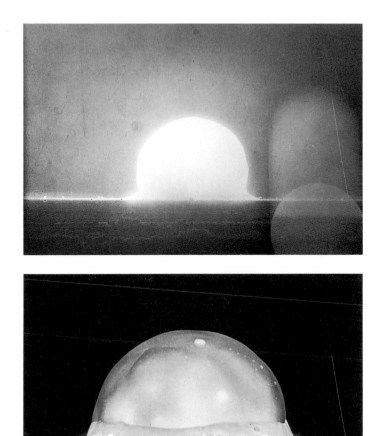

10,000 yards north.

The arrows denote an optical effect: the barrage balloon lines
appear to have broken. However, as the shock wave left the ball of
fire behind, it climbed up the cable. Light was refracted, making
the lines appear broken on the film. The cable, about to be vaporized, is only visible because it was smoking due to the extreme heat
of the blast.

Photographer: B. Brixner.
Courtesy of LANL

10,000 yards north.

In these exposures made by a Mitchell camera running at 24 fps with a wider angle lens, the intensity of the fireball has caused the top frame to solarize. Smoke expanded around the cables and two pairs of vaporized balloons can be seen at the top.

The uprush of air carried dust and hot gases up through the center of the dust skirt. The stem of the mushroom cloud was about to form.

Photographer: B. Brixner.
Courtesy of LANL

2.0 SEC.
N

⊢————⊣ 100 METERS

4.0 SEC.
N

⊢————⊣ 100 METERS

A photograph taken approximately ten seconds into the explosion, from the west, near Pope station at Trinity.

The passage of the shock wave through the upper atmosphere caused condensation and the formation of temporary clouds.

To Otto Frisch on Compaña Hill, the sudden appearance of the cloud ring reminded him of "a pool of spilt milk." Forty seconds after the explosion, many people put their fingers in their ears and Captain Larkin of the United States Navy was surprised by a sudden sound, like a "crack of thunder." Frisch heard a sound "like huge noisy waggons (sic) running around in the hills."

Photographer: Unknown.
Courtesy of LANL

This is the only color photograph taken of the Trinity explosion:
a snapshot made by SED Jack Aeby.

Photographer: Jack Aeby.

Courtesy of R. Fermi

A piece of x-ray film displaying fogged spots. Minute quantities of radioactive fallout from the Trinity test contaminated straw that was made into cardboard packing materials in Indiana in early August 1945. This straw fogged the x-ray film later packed inside it.

Courtesy of Paul W. Frame

Opposite: Aerial photograph of the Trinity site taken twenty-eight hours after detonation. Visible are zero (center), the two 800 yard stations (top and left), Jumbo (top left), and the 100-ton crater (at bottom).

Photographer: B. Waldman.

Courtesy of LANL

On July 16, 1945, the *Associated Press* reported:

"ALAMOGORDO, JULY 16 — The Commanding Officer of the Alamogordo Army Air Base made the following statement today: "Several inquires have been received concerning a heavy explosion which occurred on the Alamogordo Base reservation this morning.

A remotely located ammunition magazine containing a considerable amount of high explosives and pyrotechnics exploded. There was no loss of life or injury to anyone, and the property damage outside of the explosives magazine itself was negligible.

Weather conditions affecting the content of gas shells exploded by the blast may make it desirable for the Army to evacuate temporarily a few civilians from their homes."

Enrico Fermi in a lead-lined tank, an hour or less after the explosion, as he drove towards the crater intending to collect soil samples.
Photographer: Jack Aeby. Courtesy of R. Fermi

Remains of the
plutonium bomb's
tower.
August 1945.
Photographer: Jack Aeby.
Courtesy of Jack Aeby

Trinity site two weeks
after the explosion.
July 1945.
Photographer: E. Wallace?
Courtesy of LANL

Jumbo sat as a mute witness to the first atomic explosion. Months later, Groves ordered that a conventional explosive be detonated inside the vessel to justify Jumbo's expense. The explosives were not placed to take advantage of its special design, and both ends of Jumbo blasted apart. The central cylinder remains at Trinity site to this day. Trinity site. July 16, 1945.
Photographer: E. Wallace?
Courtesy of LANL

DELIVERY

IN A DISCUSSION ABOUT THE CHICAGO SCIENTISTS IN 1942, COLONEL

MARSHALL SAID TO THE ASSOCIATE DIRECTOR OF THE METALLURGICAL

LABORATORY, [NORMAN HILBERRY], "LOOK HILBERRY, IT SOUNDED TO ME

THAT THESE GUYS WERE SAYING THEY THINK A SINGLE BOMB,

OR TWO, IS ALL THAT'S NECESSARY . . . LET ME JUST SKETCH YOU

IN ON THE BASIC MILITARY MIND AND ETHICS AND PHILOSOPHY.

YOU NEVER USE A WEAPON THAT YOU CANNOT CONTINUE TO USE ONCE

YOU USE IT FIRST." — From *Hanford and the Bomb,* by S. L. Sanger

After the trinity test, General Farrell congratulated General Groves by saying, "The war is over," to which Groves replied, "Yes, after we drop two bombs on Japan." The Manhattan District commander immediately departed for Washington, D.C., taking a report he and Oppenheimer had written, in which they estimated the blast to be the equivalent of between 15,000 and 20,000 tons of TNT. From his paper experiment, Fermi had judged the force at closer to 15,000 tons, while later radiochemical measurements officially placed the blast at 18,600 tons. On the day of the Trinity test, President Truman and his Secretary of State, James Byrnes, on their way to Potsdam, toured Berlin's ruins. In San Francisco, the uranium bullet for the first atomic bomb left for the overseas delivery base on the island of Tinian in the Pacific.

Physicist Victor Weisskopf later remembered that he and his colleagues were ". . . too involved in the work, too deeply interested in its progress, and too dedicated to overcoming its many difficulties," to think seriously about its consequences. Niels Bohr, however, had already spent several years contemplating the nuclear arms race that was to come and he had already tried to communicate with various world leaders about post-war strategies. At the University of Chicago, the report authored by physicist James Franck called for a non-military demonstration of the atomic bomb, and Leo Szilard wrote and circulated a petition later signed by sixty-nine Met Lab scientists, claiming that if the United States dropped the bomb first it would have to "bear the responsibility of opening the door to an era of devastation on an unimaginable scale." Both Bohr and Szilard advocated international cooperation and control of the bomb, but their message ultimately fell on deaf ears.

An interim committee, advised by Manhattan Project scientists Oppenheimer, Lawrence, Fermi, and Compton, drafted the opinion that no alternative existed other than a military strike. Given the information made available to the committee by the army, this conclusion was not surprising. Although the bomb was originally conceived and designed by scientists, it was now considered a weapon for use by the military. I.I. Rabi, the physicist who was instrumental in the initial organization of the Los Alamos laboratory, explained later that the scientists had "meant well" but gave away to the military the "power" they, as the original makers of the bomb, had initially held in their hands.

The army had decided that the atomic bombs would be ready for combat use by August 1945. Target selection had begun in April, soon after Harry Truman had become President. General Groves wrote the directive for their use, specifying that the first bomb would be ready by August 3. He also contributed to the selection of targets, which ultimately were Hiroshima, Kokura, Niigata, and Nagasaki. These cities had been spared intensive Allied strategic bombing, contained military production centers, and had large populations. Groves added that additional bombs would soon be ready: a plutonium implosion bomb could be available every few weeks, while a uranium gun-design bomb could be produced every few months.

The 509th Composite Group had been formed in the spring of 1945 expressly to drop the first atomic bombs. It was led by Colonel Paul W. Tibbets and was based at Wendover Field, Utah. "Destination," was the code-name of the Pacific island of Tinian, which had recently been captured by the Americans. The bombs would be assembled and loaded into the specially designed B-29's at Destination: Little Boy was the code-name for the uranium gun-assembly device, while Fat Man was the designation for the plutonium implosion gadget.

While at Potsdam President Truman signed two documents: one was a joint declaration with Britain and the Soviet Union demanding Japan's unconditional surrender, and the other, known only to the British, was an authorization to drop the atomic bomb on Japan.

On Tinian, a special compound consisting of four air-conditioned Quonset huts in which the bombs would be assembled had been built for the newly-uniformed scientific team from Los Alamos. At the First Ordnance Technical Area, only the scientific team was permitted entry. Members of the 509th Composite Group who, during their thirteen months of training, were never told the purpose of their flight, were separated from the other American units stationed on the island. Two days before their first mission, in a tent completely surrounded by the Military Police carrying rifles, the crews were finally briefed by Captain Parsons and Colonel Tibbets on the nature of the weapon they were about to deliver. Since radar bombing was ruled out, the importance of visual bombing was stressed: the army considered it crucial to know immediately how well the new weapons worked.

Seven B-29's at Tinian were assigned to the first strike mission. Three planes were to report on weather conditions at each of the three targets; one airplane was on stand-by in Iwo Jima in case the strike plane malfunctioned. Two observation planes accompanied

A portrait of Robert Oppenheimer taken at Los Alamos by SED Mike Michnovicz, a few days after the successful Trinity test. Michnovicz was instructed to make a series of portraits of the director in anticipation of the publicity that would follow the Japan mission.
Photographer: J.J. Mike Michnovicz.
Courtesy of LANL

Below:
A portrait of Leslie Groves made on his return to Washington, D.C., immediately after the Trinity test. Ed Westcott, an Oak Ridge army photographer, was sent to photograph the General but was forced to wait several hours, during which Groves briefed officials and changed his dusty uniform. Westcott, knowing nothing about the bomb, had been instructed to picture a determined general winning the Pacific war. He asked Groves to look at the recently firebombed Tokyo. Groves declined, saying, "I'll look somewhere else." Westcott later realized that Groves had been looking directly towards Hiroshima, the atomic bomb's first target.
Photographer: E. Westcott.
Courtesy of NARA

Tibbets's *Enola Gay*, the strike aircraft. The *Enola Gay* took off at 2:45 AM on August 6, 1945, bound for Japan. The final assembly of Little Boy was completed 47,000 feet in the air by Captain Parsons because he was worried that, if the bomb were assembled prior to flight and an accident occurred, the entire island of Tinian would be destroyed. Hiroshima was the primary target and good weather was confirmed. Exactly on schedule, a high-pitched radio tone was heard in the *Enola Gay*. When it ceased, the bomb bay doors automatically opened and Little Boy was delivered.

Three days later, the second mission left Tinian island. It was beset by difficulties. The strike plane, *Bock's Car*, departed with an unusually small fuel tank, and one of the other bomber planes failed to rendezvous. Accompanied by one plane, *Bock's Car* nevertheless flew to the first target, Kokura. Three runs over the hazy city and the appearance of Japanese fighters persuaded the crew to proceed to the next target — Nagasaki. That city, too, was overcast, but the plane's critically low fuel level prevented it from making any more passes. Suddenly, the clouds broke for a moment, and Fat Man was dropped. The second weapon was far more powerful than the first, but it landed significantly off target, and the Nagasaki mountain range mitigated its impact. Its destructive effect was nevertheless immense.

In a radio address on August 15, the Japanese Emperor, whose voice most of his subjects had never heard before, announced the nation's defeat. Japan officially surrendered to the Allies that same day, and the long Second World War came to an end.

At 09:15:17 Marianas time, the first atomic bomb used in combat was dropped from an altitude of 31,600 feet. It exploded forty-five seconds later, at 08:16:02, Hiroshima time, between 1,750 and 1,900 feet above the Shima Hospital courtyard. The bomb missed its target, the Aioi Bridge, by 550 feet. The approximate yield of the bomb was 18,000 tons of TNT. The hospital and the bridge, as well as the rest of the city were instantaneously destroyed.

This photograph was taken from an observation plane by its navigator, Russell Gackenbach. The crews observed dark grey clouds nearly three miles in diameter; the mushroom cloud climbed above. Unexpectedly, two shock waves hit the plane: one from the blast and the second reflected off the ground when the fireball struck. The official photographic record of the blast was lost.

Photographer: Russell E. Gackenbach.
Courtesy of Harlow W. Russ and Robert Krauss

A Little Boy dummy
unit inside a modified
B-29 bomb bay.
Wendover Field, Utah,
c. May 1945.
Photographer: Unknown.
Courtesy of LANL

The uranium bomb
had never been
fully tested until it
was dropped on
Hiroshima.

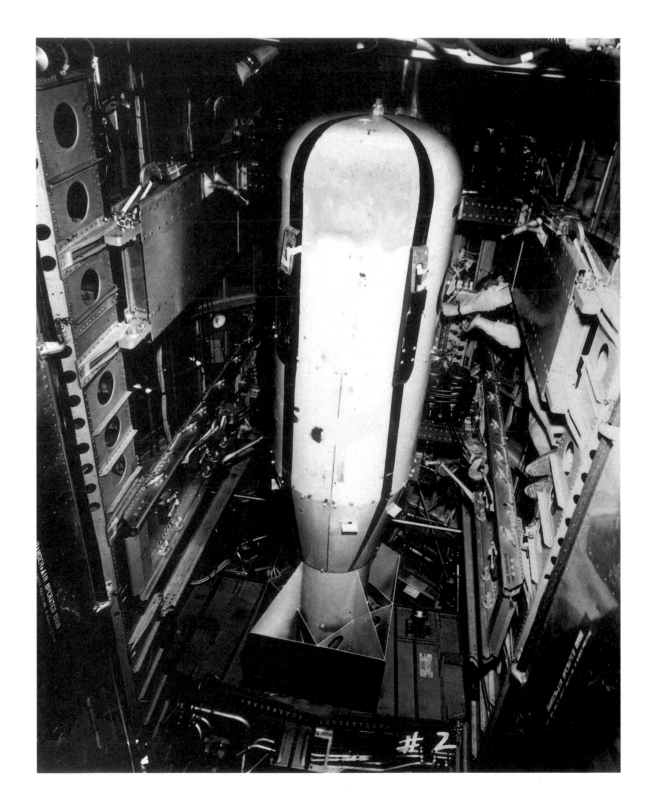

In Washington D.C., President Truman called a press conference to announce the new weapon. He threatened the Japanese with a "rain of ruin" if they failed to surrender unconditionally.

In Moscow, the Japanese Ambassador was summoned and told that the Soviet Union would now enter the war.

In Oak Ridge and Hanford, workers finally learned the secret of what they had been producing.

At Los Alamos, there was a mood of both elation and unease among the scientists about the bomb they had built.

In Tokyo, it took more than a day for the fact of the bombing to become known. The destruction in Hiroshima had cut off all communication with the outside world.

The *Enola Gay* returning from Hiroshima. Tinian, 2:58 PM, August 6, 1945. *Photographer: Unknown. Courtesy of Russell E. Gackenbach*

B-29's and the North
field airstrips.
Tinian, June–August
1945.

Photographers: Unknown.
Courtesy of Russell E.
Gackenbach

**Aerial view of Tinian,
June 1945.**
*Photographer: Unknown.
Courtesy of Russell E.
Gackenbach*

Tinian was strategically located 1,500 miles from Tokyo. After a bitter battle with the Japanese, the Allies captured the island and built a large airbase. The 20th Airforce was stationed at Tinian and the nearby islands of Guam and Saipan, from which massive bombing raids were conducted during the summer of 1945. These "strategic" raids killed many thousands of civilians and burned numerous Japanese cities.

Los Alamos physicist Philip Morrison remembered: "Tinian is a miracle. Here, 6,000 miles from San Francisco, the United States armed forces have built the largest airport in the world." He continued, "Down the great runways would roll the huge planes, seeming to move slowly because of their size, but far outspeeding the occasional racing jeep. One after another each runway would launch its planes. Once every 15 seconds another B-29 would become air-borne. For an hour and a half this would continue with precision and order. The sun would go below the sea, and the last planes could still be seen in the distance, with running lights still on. Often a plane would fail to make the take-off, and go skimming horribly into the sea, or into the beach to burn like a huge torch."

A scientific team from Los Alamos, which included Agnew, Morrison, Serber, Alvarez, Ramsey, and several SEDs, assembled the atomic bombs for the army. Overnight, they had become uniformed officers.

Agnew recounted why the bomb core is scratched out in this snapshot: "I was in Chicago after the war in 1946. The FBI came and said they believed I had some secret pictures. They went through my pictures and found nothing. Then like a fool I said, "Maybe this one is secret." They wanted to know what that thing was. I told them and then they said that must be secret and wanted the picture. I wanted the picture so they agreed if I scratched out the "thing" I could keep the slide."

Harold Agnew (right)
holding the plutonium
bomb core.
First Ordnance
Technical Area.
Tinian, August, 1945.
Photographer: Unknown
Courtesy of Harold M.
Agnew

Clockwise from top:

**Members of the
509th group on
Tinian, c. August 1945.**
*Photographer: Charles
Levy.*
Courtesy of Charles Levy

**Bombardier Charles
Levy in full flying
gear, c. August 1945.**
*Photographer: Charles
Levy.*
Courtesy of Charles Levy

**Army Captain
Frederick Bock seated
in *Bock's Car*,
c. August 1945.**
*Photographer: Charles
Levy.*
Courtesy of Charles Levy

**Bernard Waldman?,
a member of the
scientific group on
Tinian, August 1945.**
Photographer: Unknown.
Courtesy of LANL

Left, from top:

William Laurence (*New York Times* science reporter), Henry Barnett (physician), and Robert Serber (physicist), outside their living quarters on Tinian, **August 1945.**

Photographer: William Penney.

Courtesy of Robert Serber

Guarded entrance to First Ordinance Technical Area. Tinian, July 1945.

Photographer: Unknown.

Courtesy of Russell E. Gackenbach

Shot-out Japanese tank. Tinian, July 1, 1945.

Photographer: Harlow W. Russ.

Courtesy of Harlow W. Russ

Above:

Shinto Shrine located in one of the primary combat areas during the battle for Tinian, July 1, 1945.

Photographer: Harlow W. Russ.

Courtesy of Harlow W. Russ

The drop testing that had been conducted at Wendover continued even after the 509th group reached Tinian. Real targets in Japan were now selected for the 5,500 pounds of high explosives. They were called "pumpkin" missions, because the bombs were painted orange.

A "pumpkin bomb" dedicated to a fraternity brother of Charles Levy's who was killed in the Bataan Death March. *Photographer: Charles Levy.*
Courtesy of Charles Levy

Aerial view of a dummy Fat Man bomb falling over Nakajima, Japan, July 29, 1945.

Photographer: Unknown.

Courtesy of Charles Levy

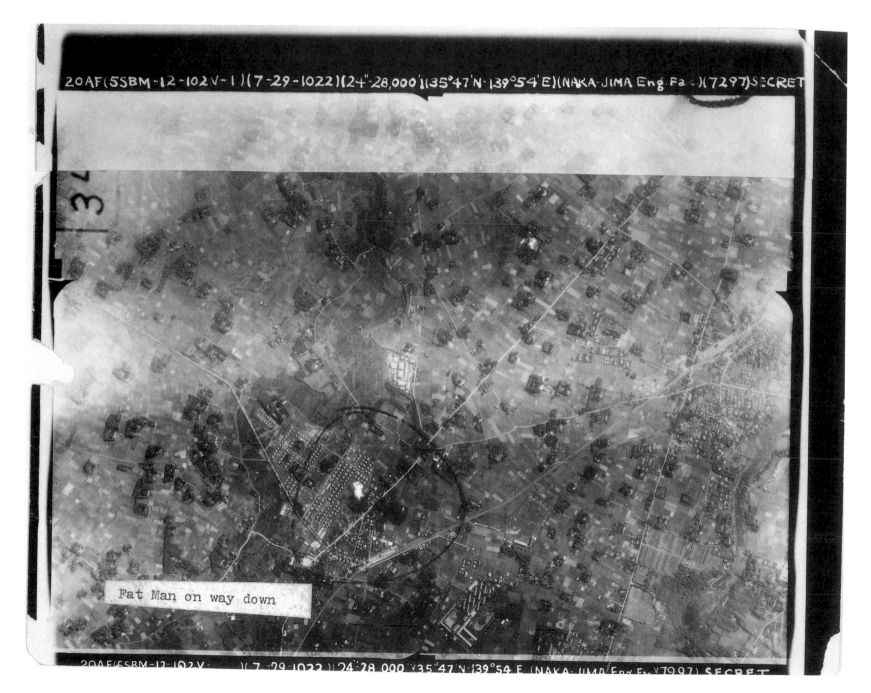

20AF(5SBM-12-102V-1)(7-29-1022)(24"-28,000')(35°47'N-139°54'E)(NAKA-JIMA Eng Fa-)(7297)SECRET

Fat Man on way down

20AF(5SBM-12-102V-)(7-29-1022)(24-28,000'X35°47'N-139°54'E (NAKA-JIMA Eng Fa-)(7997) SECRET

A tool kit for the final assembly of the Fat Man bomb. *Photographer: Unknown. Courtesy of LANL*

The original date for dropping the second bomb was August 11, but a forecast of bad weather moved the mission forward to August 9. The assembly of the Fat Man bomb was so complex that it required four teams of scientists and technicians to assemble the high explosives, the plutonium core, the firing system, and the fusing devices, which constituted the bomb inside of its ballistic casing.

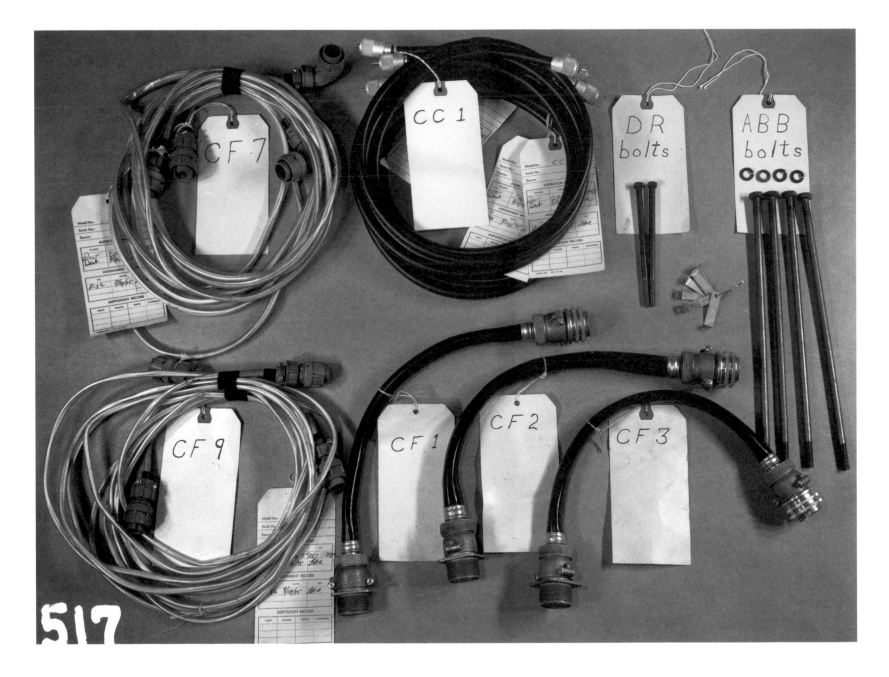

**Fat Man unit F-31.
Tinian, August 8,
1945.**
*Photographer: Unknown.
Courtesy of LANL*

Fusing, firing, and
cabling systems were
checked before the
nose cap, the last part
of the ballistic case,
was installed. By 8:00
PM the bomb had been
loaded into the belly
of *Bock's Car.*

The second atomic bomb used in combat exploded 1,650 feet above Nagasaki after falling for approximately forty-seven seconds, at 11:02 AM on August 9, 1945. Its force was later estimated at 21,000 tons of TNT, ±10%. The bomb exploded more than one mile from its target, hitting the Mitsubishi Steel and Arms Works in the north of the city. Five shock waves hit the planes. Not taken into account was the fact that the mountains running through Nagasaki would act as reflectors of the blast.

Robert Serber had been thrown off the observation plane minutes before take-off because one parachute was missing. The purpose of sending this plane was to officially record and calculate the yield of the explosion with a Fastax camera that only Serber knew how to operate. The physicist was left to walk the three miles back to base alone. Bombardier Charles Levy, with his own small camera, took a series of snapshots of the explosion.

A third bomb would soon be ready to be shipped to Tinian, but it was canceled when President Truman issued the orders to halt the atomic bombings on August 10. Japan formally surrendered on August 15. Tinian and Los Alamos, however, were both required to maintain a "state of readiness" during the negotiations.

Photographer: Charles Levy.

Courtesy of Charles Levy

A FEARFUL SILENCE

THE PEOPLE OF HIROSHIMA were just beginning their workday when the first atomic bomb was dropped. When the second bomb fell on Nagasaki three days later, its inhabitants, also unaware of the new weapon, were equally unprepared for its effects. One moment people were living ordinary lives; in the next, life had practically ceased.

In each city, the heat soared to millions of degrees centigrade at the epicenter of the blasts. On the ground, the estimated temperature in both hypocenters was 3,000° to 4,000° C. People, animals, insects, and plants were instantly killed by the intense heat. Most people within a mile of ground zero were charred beyond recognition, while those within four kilometers suffered intense thermal burns. The harsh brightness of the bomb's flash photographically etched the shadowy contours of people, plants, and objects permanently into hard stone.

The bomb's blast, its sheer force, smashed buildings, bridges, and roads. Reinforced steel columns snapped; the Mitsubishi Steel and Arms Works were flattened. The wind could be felt eleven kilometers away and literally pulled people apart. Many died when they were crushed by parts of buildings or pieces of their own furniture flying in the air. Those who could crawl out from underneath the rubble found their skin carved by shards of glass.

Violent fire storms broke out within half an hour after each bomb exploded. The wind blew fiercely for several hours, fanning flames and destroying nearly everything within two kilometers. After the fires, radioactive "black rain" was produced by carbon ash rising into the cold air and combining with water vapor.

Radioactivity was emitted both from the burst point and from fission fragments on the ground. Although they were dropped from the air to minimize fallout, the bombs released deadly gamma rays which killed and injured those close to the hypocenter, both at the moment of impact and in the hours and days afterwards. Reports of a strange malady, which afflicted people who were not otherwise apparently injured or near to the hypocenter when the bombs were dropped, began to circulate in the following days and weeks. Symptoms included bleeding gums, skin spots, epilation, and inexplicable fatigue: all indicative of what became known as radiation sickness.

By the end of 1945 it is estimated that the dead numbered approximately 140,000 in Hiroshima and 70,000 in Nagasaki.

On August 12, 1945, General Groves ordered a Manhattan District scientific group to travel to Hiroshima and Nagasaki, ". . . with the first American troops in order that these troops shall not be subjected to any possible toxic effects although we have no reason to believe that any such effects actually exist." Groves had no intention of giving credence to the increasing number of press stories regarding radiation illness.

The Manhattan Project Atomic Bomb Investigating Group was to measure existing radiation levels, assess the physical effects of the bombs, and secure intelligence information concerning Japan's prior effort to build an atomic bomb. Its members arrived at the beginning of September and were among the first westerners to walk through the bleak and blasted Japanese wastelands. Preliminary inspections were made at Hiroshima on September 8th and 9th; in Nagasaki on September 13th and 14th. Because the team found no unusual levels of radiation on the ground, U.S. troops immediately began their occupation of the defeated cities.

The following photographs were all taken by the physicist Robert Serber, one of the earliest arrivals at Los Alamos, and one of the few scientists to witness, first hand, the devastating physical effects of the weapon he had helped to build. The scale and import of his work in Japan was dramatically different from that done only weeks before, analyzing blast data from Trinity's desert floor. Now, Serber and the other Manhattan Project physicists searched for detailed evidence of how their "gadget" had worked on a once human landscape.

The Manhattan Project would officially run for another year, until after the Navy's very public Operation Crossroads in the Bikini atolls. For most of the scientists, though, the desolation of the two Japanese cities, so sharply observed by Serber, marked the uneasy close of the first, secret chapter of the atomic era.

Nagasaki.
First floor of the
Administration
Building.

Photographer: Robert
Serber.
Courtesy of LANL

**Hiroshima,
600 feet east of zero.**
*Photographer: Robert
Serber.
Courtesy of LANL*

Nagasaki,
1,400 feet north of
zero. The Mitsubishi
Steel and Arms Works.

Photographer: Robert
Serber.
Courtesy of Robert
Serber

Hiroshima,
2,400 feet north-east of
zero.

Photographer: Robert
Serber.
Courtesy of Robert Serber

"SOME PEOPLE HAD MANY STREAKS OF CLOTTED BLOOD ON THEIR FACES AND LIMBS, THE BLOOD ALREADY DRIED. SOME WERE STILL BLEEDING; THEIR FACES, HANDS, AND LEGS WERE DRIPPING BLOOD. BY NOW, ALL THE FACES, TOO, HAD BEEN HIDEOUSLY TRANSFORMED . . . VIRTUALLY EVERYONE WAS NAKED TO THE WAIST . . . THEIR BODIES WERE DISTENDED, LIKE THE BODIES OF PEOPLE WHO HAVE DROWNED. THEIR FACES WERE FAT AND ENORMOUSLY PUFFED UP. THEIR EYES WERE SWOLLEN SHUT, AND THE SKIN AROUND THEIR EYES WAS CRINKLY AND PINK. THEY HELD THEIR PUFFY SWOLLEN ARMS, BENT AT THE ELBOWS, IN FRONT OF THEM, MUCH LIKE CRABS WITH TWO CLAWS. AND HANGING DOWN FROM BOTH ARMS LIKE RAGS WAS GRAY-COLORED SKIN . . . ONE COULDN'T SEE THEIR EYES. EVEN THOUGH THESE PEOPLE WERE IN SUCH FRIGHTFUL SHAPE, NOWHERE DID PANDEMONIUM ARISE. NOR DID THE TERM HARROWING APPLY. FOR EVERYONE WAS SILENT." — Yoko Ota, Hiroshima

"... THE AIR FLASHED A BRILLIANT YELLOW AND THERE WAS A HUGE BLAST OF WIND ... LATER, WHEN I CAME TO MY SENSES, I NOTICED A HOLE HAD BEEN BLOWN IN THE ROOF, ALL THE GLASS HAD BEEN SHATTERED, AND THAT THE GLASS HAD CUT MY SHOULDER AND I WAS BLEEDING. WHEN I WENT OUTSIDE, THE SKY HAD TURNED FROM BLUE TO BLACK AND THE BLACK RAIN STARTED TO FALL ... ALL THAT I KNEW HAD DISAPPEARED. ONLY THE CONCRETE AND IRON SKELETONS OF THE BUILDINGS REMAINED. THERE WERE DEAD BODIES EVERYWHERE. ON EACH STREET CORNER WE HAD TUBS OF WATER USED FOR PUTTING OUT FIRES AFTER THE AIR RAIDS. IN ONE OF THESE SMALL TUBS, SCARCELY LARGE ENOUGH FOR ONE PERSON, WAS THE BODY OF A DESPERATE MAN WHO HAD SOUGHT COOL WATER. THERE WAS FOAM COMING FROM HIS MOUTH, BUT HE WAS NOT ALIVE." — Michito Ichimaru, Nagasaki

Japan at War: An Oral History

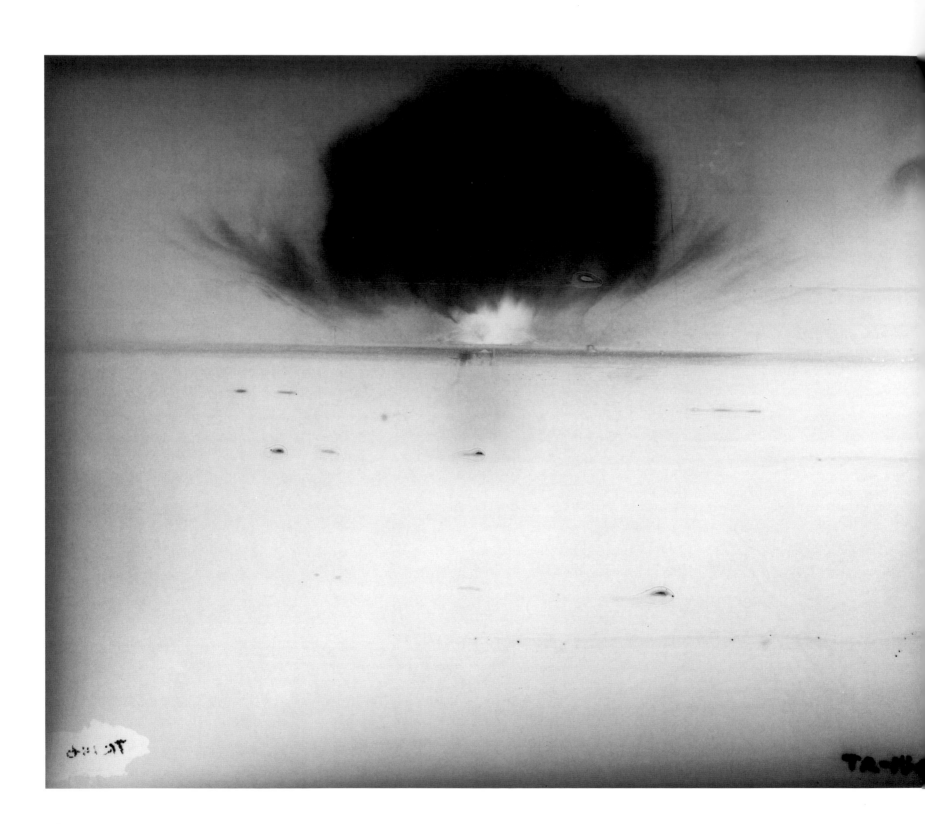

AFTERWORD

BY ESTHER SAMRA

T HE UNSETTLING WORLD OF THE Manhattan Project was photographed without design. So many different people photographed so many different locations and activities within the Manhattan District between 1942 and 1946 that the resulting photographic record is both varied and voluminous.

Hundreds of thousands of photographs were taken by the individuals who lived and worked within the rigorous confines of the Manhattan Engineering District, yet most of us associate the secret project with just one image — that of the mushroom cloud, which has become an icon of mass destruction in our culture. In most history books, the same few photographs are often repeated as illustrations. Once one begins, though, to look at the many kinds of photographic imagery produced from *within* the Manhattan District, as we did when we began this work, certain questions arise: what did this world feel like from the inside, and how was it seen by those insiders for themselves? How was it portrayed to the outside world? Was there one unified Manhattan Project, or were there many distinct facets? These questions have guided us through the territory marked by the thousands of images, hundreds of people, scores of sites, and dozens of books relating to the making of the first atomic bombs.

The origin of this particular book was personal: Rachel Fermi was given a box of family photographs, including images from past travels and holidays. Within this box she found, and was struck by, one small, faded photograph of the Trinity explosion. The juxtaposition of family snapshots and this image of an atomic blast was startling. The photograph was itself perplexing: its frayed edges and pale red color lent a vulnerability to the print which was in stark contrast to the powerful nature of the explosion it recorded. Later, we found that the photograph, taken by Jack Aeby, a member of Emilio Segrè's

group, was one of the very few snapshots taken of the Trinity blast, and the only one made in color. The discovery of this snapshot, and of other images of Enrico Fermi at Los Alamos, intrigued us sufficiently to wonder about the photographs that had been taken and collected by other Manhattan Project participants.

We became interested in seeing how these personal images coexisted with the official record. The snapshots seen in this book extend the existing official documentation and enable us to view the Manhattan Project as a complex historical event. The photographs don't explain why the first atomic bombs were made, or provide a comprehensive history. Rather, they point to the complexity of this event by virtue of the many means photography has at its disposal to document human activity.

The varied nature of the photographic material from the Manhattan Project may be identified and looked at discretely — to a certain extent. In one category are the photographs that document the scientific work. Oddly enough, during the first significant experiment of the Manhattan Project, i.e., the Chicago chain reaction on December 2, 1942, no photographs were taken. Several images of the pile being built, an artistic rendering of the actual event, and a motion picture reenactment, are the only surviving testimonials. This example reminds us of the many other photographs that could have been, but which were not, taken during the Manhattan Project, in addition to those that remain classified, or which were lost or destroyed for reasons of security and control. We cannot suppose in many cases what these may have been, but their absence reinforces the idea that no record, photographic or written, is complete; and

Pinhole image of the Trinity test. Four second exposure. Trinity site, July 16, 1945.
Photographer: J. Mack. Courtesy of LANL

From top:

**Berlyn Brixner,
an SED in the Optics
Group photographing
a drop test, probably
at Wendover, Utah.
Project A, 1945.
Brixner became leader
of the Optics Group
in the fall of 1945 after
Julian Mack left
Los Alamos.**
Photographer: Unknown.
Courtesy of LANL

**Drop test photographs
of a Fat Man ballistic
shape, probably at
Muroc Bombing
Range, California.
Project A, 1945.**
Photographer: B. Brixner.
Courtesy of LANL

**Interior of a camera
bunker at 10,000
yards.
Trinity site, 1945.**
Photographer: Unknown.
Courtesy of LANL

that any documentation presented to the public is always an interpretation of available information.

The Optical Group at Los Alamos numbered about a dozen scientists, photographers, and SEDs, and was led by the physicist Julian Mack. The group served the needs of the scientists, who often required visual data to judge the success of their work. Events which were previously thought nearly impossible to photograph were now captured successfully: for example, high-speed implosion experiments which sometimes exceeded 15,000 frames per second, and an analysis of the Trinity explosion which alone comprised hundreds of thousands of images. When they were first made, these photographs were used primarily as evidence. Now some of them, particularly those from Trinity, have accrued a meaning over and beyond that of scientific data: they have entered the matrix of contemporary culture.

By necessity, the Optical Group adapted current photographic technology to its particular needs. Some of the cameras Julian Mack and his talented assistant Berlyn Brixner procured were ordinary cameras, others had been invented by the engineer Harold Edgerton at M.I.T. In almost all instances, the cameras had to be modified to perform their specific function (for instance, an adapted Hollywood motion picture camera was used to photograph the Trinity explosion). In their search for photographic means whereby experimentation could be documented accurately, the Optical Group contributed new technologies. After the war, Berlyn Brixner developed a rotating slit mirror camera that operated at fifteen million frames per second. Other ideas were shared with Edgerton, who used them himself soon afterward to photograph nuclear and other kinds of high speed explosions.

Julian Mack spent the weeks before the Trinity test organizing his photographic instrumentation and devising myriad photographic experiments. In addition to placing complex photographic devices at the bunkers 800 and 10,000 yards from ground zero, Mack also had made the most elementary kind of photograph — the pinhole. He was curious, Brixner has explained, to see the explosion in as many photographic dimensions as possible.

This was photography done in the service of science. A range of other kinds of photography was also practiced in the course of the Manhattan Project. The army, and construction and industrial companies, recorded the building of sites, but many of the activities that occurred within them, because of the secret nature of the project, were not documented. The companies that did photograph their work — Du Pont, which built and operated Hanford; the Zia company, which constructed the Los Alamos laboratory; the architectural firm Skidmore, Owings & Merrill, whose first large commission was the housing at Oak Ridge; and Allis-Chalmers, which manufactured the pumps for the K-25 plant and the magnetic coils for the Y 12 plant — generated an invaluable record of how the Manhattan District used huge resources to initiate what we now call the nuclear weapons industry.

At each of the two MED manufacturing sites — Oak Ridge and Hanford — public relations photography played a conspicuous role, and was used by the army to control information. Each town had a local paper and carried stories of interest to its citizens, such as marriages, births, openings of schools and theaters, accidents, etc. The roving photographers of Oak Ridge, Hanford, and Los Alamos, who were hired by the army or industry, Ed Westcott, Robley Johnson, and Mike Michnovicz, respectively, spent the official years of the Manhattan Project photographing an impressive array of subjects and events. Westcott made more than 10,000 negatives that are now housed at the National Archives in Washington, D.C., and photographed everything from the initial construction of the city of Oak Ridge to official portraits of important staff personnel and factory interiors. Neither he nor Robley Johnson, who was hired by Du Pont, were reporters in any real sense, since they were ultimately told by the army what to photograph. Much of their versatile work stands as a symbol of how public and private worlds intersected in the Manhattan Project. These photographers used the camera, which is a means of making something public, to document secret activities within a private world. In many respects that world has a veneer which looks and feels familiar to us, yet we know now, looking in from the outside, that the familiarity is deceptive.

Vernacular photography from the Manhattan Project extends the notion that prosaic photographs can capture an extraordinary world. Cameras, like guns, were considered potential weapons and had to be deposited with security personnel at each of the three sites. At Los Alamos, the security handbook specified how cameras were to be used: "No photographs will be made of the following subjects," the handbook read, "any building or installation on the Post, except unidentifiable portions thereof. Any equipment, material or signs. Photographs of personnel other than that of the sender's immediate family." The snapshot evidence, particularly from Los Alamos, demonstrates that these restrictions were not always followed to the letter. A surprising amount of unofficial snapshot pho-

Self-portrait of Robley L. Johnson, Du Pont photographer for a *Sage Sentinel* feature entitled "Rob Johnson in Action."
January 5, 1945.
Photographer: R. Johnson.
Courtesy of the DOE

Middle, left:
Self-portrait of SED Mike Michnovicz, army photographer in the Photographic Group.
Los Alamos, 1945.
Photographer: J.J. Mike Michnovicz.
Courtesy of J.J. Mike Michnovicz

Middle, right:
Public relations photograph, "Sunday Punch," a B-25 bomber, given to the Army Airforce by the K-25 workers from Oak Ridge.
March 15, 1945.
Photographer: E. Westcott.
Courtesy of NARA

Bottom:
Self-portrait of Ed Westcott, Army Corps of Engineers photographer, in his darkroom.
Oak Ridge, 1945.
Photographer: E. Westcott.
Courtesy of NARA

**Guns and cameras
checked at a guard
post.
Oak Ridge, c. 1944.**
Photographer: E. Westcott.
Courtesy of NARA

tography exists, in contrast to the more rigid, formal, and controlled official photographs the Manhattan District released after its secret was revealed to the public.

Information emerges in the snapshot photography that is missing in the other forms of photography undertaken during the Manhattan District. The representation of hierarchies, particularly at Los Alamos, comes across clearly in the snapshots, as does the encounter between the worlds of the Anglos and Indians. The snapshot images, whether from Los Alamos, Oak Ridge, Hanford, Tinian, or Japan, create an eerie sort of family album of an experience which pushes the limits of human activity.

On Tinian, the official military photography generated from within the 509th Composite Group coexists with snapshots taken by the crews of the two Japanese missions, and the Manhattan District team. Though each mission had an official photographic instrumentation plane which flew alongside the strike aircraft, certain problems prevented either of them from producing much photographic information. On the Hiroshima mission, the film that was made was either destroyed during processing at Tinian or lost. On the Nagasaki flight, physicist Robert Serber — the only person who knew how to operate the Fastax camera — was left behind. Though radio contact was reluctantly made with the instrumentation plane, the camera was evidently too complex for anyone on board to operate. Incredibly enough, almost all the surviving photographs depicting the explosions of the atomic bombs over Japan were snapshots taken by the strike crew members themselves.

The best-known photograph of the Nagasaki mushroom cloud, which has been reprinted countless times in the last fifty years, was taken by Bombardier Charles Levy with his own camera. Levy and the other crew members had been given permission to use their own cameras on the strike missions (the photographs were inspected by the army after processing). After returning to the United States, Levy lost his negatives, but gave his photographs to a major magazine that used them without attribution, and sold them to other news organizations.

When they actually landed on Japanese soil several weeks later, the Manhattan District team used their cameras to record evidence of the bomb's destructive capability. The hundreds of photographs of blast and heat damage that were made were later incorporated into a classified report written by the Manhattan District team, while images of the human tragedy were made primarily by the Japanese in the days after the bombs struck. The Manhattan District photographs have become part of the official record depicting the damage wrought by the first atomic bombs, but the whereabouts of the original negatives is still unknown. It is common knowledge that General Groves exercised great control over the dissemination of Manhattan District photographs of Japan after the bombs were dropped. Harold Agnew, who flew with the *Great Artiste* on the Hiroshima mission, and who was responsible for retrieving the motion picture film, has recounted a cat-and-mouse chase across the Pacific, as he tried, and ultimately succeeded in, keeping the film out of Groves's hands (it is now at the Hoover Institution at Stanford University). For several weeks beforehand, Ed Westcott at Oak Ridge was busy making press kits that included photographs of important District sites, factories, and personnel. The images of segregated housing included in this book were also made at that time, in anticipation, it appears, of questions reporters might ask. They were printed in the Black newspapers of the time, such as the *Chicago Defender* and the *Washington Afro-American.*

A discernible tension between the official and the unofficial, the public and the private, and what is kept secret or revealed runs through the photographs from the Manhattan Engineering District. This is felt nowhere more keenly than in the photography album pages that begin and end this book, particularly the page belonging to Robert and Charlotte Serber. These two individuals, who were deeply involved participants in the Manhattan Project, made an album that documented their experience. It contains dozens of small black and white snapshots from Los Alamos glued on pages that have yellowed and become brittle over the years. Even holding the album is a reminder of time's impact, as it literally crumbles when the pages are turned. There are many photographs from Hiroshima and Nagasaki in the album, strange souvenirs of Serber's sojourn, but the very personal experience of being among the first outsiders to walk in a world altered by the atomic bomb is too great for the still photograph to capture. In the other family album, the Critchfield's child is learning to walk in the world being changed by his father and other scientists. Both of them, the adult and the child, like all the other people and landscapes in this book, move poignantly from the old world to the new, transformed by the invention of the atomic bomb.

Harold Agnew holding the Nagasaki bomb core. Tinian, August 1945.

Photographer: Unknown. Courtesy of Harold M. Agnew

BIOGRAPHIES AND PROFILES

Hans Bethe

I.D. badge photograph. Los Alamos, 1943.

Photographer: Unknown. Courtesy of LANL

Hans Bethe was one of several key physicists whom Oppenheimer persuaded to join the Los Alamos laboratory, where he became the head of the Theoretical Division. Bethe, born in Alsace-Lorraine in 1906, was educated in Germany and emigrated to the United States in 1935 to teach at Cornell University. After the war, Bethe returned to Cornell, where he is professor emeritus of Physics and of Nuclear Studies. Bethe won the Nobel Prize in physics in 1967 for his work on energy production in stars.

British Mission

Party held for the Los Alamos staff after the war, hosted by the British Mission.

Fuller Lodge, September 1945.

Photographer: J.J. Mike Michnovicz.

Courtesy of J.J. Mike Michnovicz

The British Mission was a part of the Anglo-American collaboration on the atomic bomb. Twenty-one British experimental physicists arrived at Los Alamos in December 1943, including Sir James Chadwick, Rudolf Peierls, Otto Frisch, James Tuck, William Penney, and Ernest Titterton. Two Canadians, George Placzek and Carson Mark, were also members of the delegation. The 1943 Quebec agreement had established the terms on which the British and Canadians would participate with the Americans: full exchange of information was to be limited and defined only by what was necessary for the war effort. The leader of the British Mission, James Chadwick, was the only member who was fully informed about the details of the Manhattan District.

Charles Critchfield

At a party in Los Alamos, 1946.

Photographer: J.J. Mike Michnovicz. Courtesy of LANL

In 1943, Charles and Jean Critchfield arrived in Los Alamos, where Charles was one of the laboratory's original group leaders and made significant contributions to the development of the Little Boy bomb. After the laboratory reorganization in 1944, Critchfield worked in the initiator group and was responsible for developing the Urchin initiator for the Fat Man bomb. One of the Critchfield's four children was born at Los Alamos during the war years. After the war, Critchfield taught physics and later returned to Los Alamos as an associate division leader. He died in 1994.

Enola Gay

North Field, Tinian, August 1945.

Photographer: Unknown. Courtesy of LANL

The 509th Composite Group was created especially by the U.S. Army Air Corps to drop the atomic bombs over Japan. The combat group was based at Wendover Field, Utah, and for a short time in Cuba. The group numbered 225 officers and 1,542 enlisted men. Its commanding officer was Colonel Paul W. Tibbets. On the afternoon of August 5, 1945, Robert Lewis, who normally flew the B-29, number 82 airplane, found the name of Tibbets's mother, Enola Gay, painted on its side.

Enrico Fermi

Lake Michigan, 1946.

Photographer: Leona Marshall Libby. Courtesy of J. Marshall

Enrico Fermi was born in Rome, Italy, in 1901, where his distinguished career in physics began. At the age of 25, he became a full professor of theoretical physics and in 1928, he married Laura Capon (who later became a writer). In 1929, the Royal Academy of Italy elected him as its youngest member. During the 1930s, Fermi's experiments with slow neutrons led the Nobel committee to give him the 1938 prize in physics. After travelling to Stockholm to accept the award, Fermi and his family escaped fascist Italy by secretly emigrating to the United States.

At Columbia University in New York, Fermi began work with Leo Szilard to demonstrate the first self-sustaining nuclear chain reaction. The experiment was later moved to the University of Chicago, where Fermi achieved the historic chain reaction on December 2, 1942.

Fermi arrived at Los Alamos in 1944, where he became the Associate Director of the laboratory, and had a division named after him. His unusual dual expertise in theoretical and experimental physics enabled him to work on many different kinds of problems for the Manhattan Project. After the war, Fermi returned to the University of Chicago, where he studied nuclear particles, and in 1946 he was awarded the Congressional Medal of Merit. In 1954, the Enrico Fermi Award was established in his honor. In that same year, he died of cancer.

General Leslie R. Groves

Oak Ridge, c. 1945.

Photographer: E. Westcott. Courtesy of NARA

Leslie Groves was born in 1896 and attended West Point. In 1931 he was chief of supply in the Office of Engineers in Washington, D.C. It was in this capacity that Groves supervised the construction of the Pentagon. After reluctantly accepting command of the Manhattan Engineering District in 1942, Groves traveled frequently across the United States selecting sites, recruiting industries, and organizing tens of thousands of workers to build the atomic bomb. His successful completion of the project won him promotion to Brigadier General in 1945, and to Major General three years later. In 1948 he retired from the army and later worked for Remington Rand. He died in 1970.

E.O. Lawrence

Inspecting the arrival of the first crane rail for the 184-inch cyclotron.

Berkeley, May 13, 1942.

Photographer: Donald Cooksey.

Courtesy of the Lawrence Berkeley Laboratory

Ernest Orlando Lawrence, born in 1901, is best known as the inventor of the cyclotron. Lawrence's cyclotron was a powerful particle accelerator which disintegrated atomic nuclei, produced artificial isotopes (later useful in medicine), and created new elements, such as plutonium. At the age of thirty-five, Lawrence became director of the Radiation Laboratory at Berkeley (known today as the Lawrence Berkeley Laboratory), and in 1939 he won the Nobel Prize in physics. Lawrence championed the electromagnetic separation process, based on the principles of the cyclotron and the mass spectrograph, and convinced General Groves to use it as one of the primary means of separating uranium.

After the war, Lawrence was involved in the government decision to develop the hydrogen bomb. This pitted him against his old friend, Robert Oppenheimer, who opposed it. With Edward Teller, Lawrence founded the Livermore National Laboratory. He died in 1958.

John and Leona Marshall

Chicago, c. 1942.

Photographer: Enrico Fermi. Courtesy of J. Marshall

John and Leona Marshall were young physicists at the University of Chicago who worked on the first chain reaction. They subsequently went to Hanford, where both worked on the development and operation of the plutonium reactors. They returned to the University of Chicago after the war, where they worked with Fermi. After the Marshalls divorced, each held teaching and research posts and returned individually to work at Los Alamos. Leona Marshall Libby, who had been one of the few female physicists in the Manhattan Project, died in 1986.

The Metallurgical Laboratory, Instrumentation Section, University of Chicago
December 30, 1944.

Photographer: Unknown. Courtesy of Ron Kathren

The Metallurgical Laboratory, or Met Lab, was the code-name devised for the research laboratory at the University of Chicago that studied the fundamental physics for a nuclear chain reaction and the production of plutonium. In January 1942, physics department chairman Arthur Holly Compton, who was also responsible for theoretical studies and bomb design for the Manhattan District, selected his university as the Project's initial primary research site. After Los Alamos was established in 1943, and the work on bomb design moved to New Mexico, the Chicago laboratory continued other kinds of related research. The Health Physics Group was an example. Its Instrumentation Section was responsible for developing radiation monitoring equipment, such as dosimeters, geiger counters, and portable survey meters, that were used both during the Manhattan Project and after the war.

Members of the National Defense Research Committee (NDRC)
From left to right, E.O. Lawrence, A.H. Compton, V. Bush, J.B. Conant, K. Compton, and A. Loomis, discussing the proposed cyclotron at the University of California at Berkeley.

Photographer: Unknown. Courtesy of NARA

The NDRC was established in 1940 by the United States government at the suggestion of Vannevar Bush, the president of the Carnegie Institution, to coordinate scientific research during the Second World War. It was later incorporated into a larger agency, the Office of Scientific Research and Development (or OSRD), which oversaw scientific and engineering research. Two of its best-known projects were the M.I.T. radar program and S-1, the original code-name for the Manhattan Project.

Colonel Kenneth D. Nichols
Oak Ridge, 1945.

Photographer: Unknown. Courtesy of the Army Corps of Engineers

Over 700,000 officers, or eight percent of the World War Two Army, were members of the United States Army Corps of Engineers. Between the summer of 1940 and 1945, eleven billion dollars was spent on various construction projects ranging from the Pentagon building to airfields, hospitals, and storage depots in the United States and abroad. The Secretary of War, General Stimson, ordered the Corps of Engineers to create an engineering district in 1942 to oversee the huge construction projects necessary to build an atomic bomb. Colonel Kenneth D. Nichols, the deputy District Engineer, was involved in the project even before General Groves was appointed Chief Engineer. The district's first location, in lower Manhattan, was the source of the project's code-name: the Manhattan Engineering District, or the Manhattan Project.

J. Robert Oppenheimer

Washington, D.C., 1945.

Photographer: Unknown. Courtesy of Peter Oppenheimer

J. Robert Oppenheimer, born in New York City in 1904, studied science and classical languages at Harvard and received his Ph.D. in physics from Gottingen, Germany. Oppenheimer took up posts at the University of California at Berkeley and at the California Institute of Technology, where he achieved a reputation as a sharp and charismatic teacher. Oppenheimer had already begun thinking about the atomic bomb when General Groves approached him to work on the Manhattan Project. He was the director of the Los Alamos laboratory from April 1943 until October 1946. After Hiroshima, Oppenheimer became one of America's most prominent figures. He was a member of many government committees, including the General Advisory Committee for the civilian Atomic Energy Commission, and he spoke often about atomic weapons and American defense policy. In 1947, Oppenheimer moved to the Institute of Advanced Study in Princeton. In 1954, during the McCarthy era, Oppenheimer's loyalty to the United States was questioned, both because of his sympathies in the 1930s with left-wing groups and because of his opposition to the hydrogen bomb. After a hearing, his security clearance was revoked by the Personnel Security Board and the Atomic Energy Commission. Oppenheimer then returned to Princeton, where he wrote and taught until the end of his life. According to his Manhattan Project colleague Rudolf Peierls, Oppenheimer spoke about the cancer that killed him in 1967 "as lucidly as about a conclusion in physics."

The Roane-Anderson women's softball team

Oak Ridge, c. 1946.

Photographer: E. Westcott. Courtesy of NARA

The Roane-Anderson company, named after the two surrounding counties of Oak Ridge, ran the city for the Army Corps of Engineers. There were so many representatives of various American industries at Oak Ridge that baseball and softball teams regularly played one another after work on fields built especially for them.

Robinette daughters

Wheat Community, Tennessee, 1939.

Photographer: Unknown. Courtesy of the Tennessee Valley Authority

Beginning in 1933, the Tennessee Valley Authority hired a staff of photographers to document its vast construction activities and the people, mostly farmers, who lived in the region. One of the larger areas was known as the Wheat Community. In 1942, the people inhabiting this area were forcibly moved and their land confiscated by the military in order to construct the Clinton Engineering Works (also known as Oak Ridge) for the Manhattan District.

San Ildefonso couple

San Ildefonso Pueblo, 1945.

Photographer: M. Kolodney. Courtesy of M. Kolodney

The San Ildefonso Pueblo lies several miles from Los Alamos, near the sacred Black Mesa. The Indians who lived in the pueblo (the well-known sculptor Maria Martinez and husband José among them), were changed by their proximity to the Los Alamos laboratory. After the war, several local anthropologists suggested that the Indians were corrupted by modern conveniences and customs. Bernice Brode, however, disagreed: "Most of us felt that many Indians were tired of being pressured to remain so traditional for the benefit of tourists and even their well-wishers."

Emilio Segrè

Los Alamos, c. 1945.

Photographer: Unknown. Courtesy of LANL

Emilio Segrè, born in 1905, was one of Fermi's students, and held posts at the Universities of Rome and Palermo before emigrating to the United States in 1940. After his arrival in America, he taught at the University of California at Berkeley, where he worked with the group that discovered plutonium. At Los Alamos, Segrè was the leader of the Radioactivity Group. Their discovery of the spontaneous fission of plutonium led to the complete reorganization of the Los Alamos laboratory in the summer of 1944. After the war, he held teaching posts at Berkeley and the University of Rome. In 1959, together with Owen Chamberlain, he received the Nobel Prize for the discovery of the antiproton. He died in 1989.

Robert and Charlotte Serber

Los Alamos, c. 1944.

Photographer: Unknown. Courtesy of Robert R. Wilson

Robert Serber, born in 1909, was a student of Oppenheimer's at Berkeley and accompanied him to Los Alamos. Both Serbers worked in the Technical Area: Robert was a group leader and introduced scientists arriving at Los Alamos to the current state of atomic research with a series of lectures called the primer. Charlotte, as the only female group leader, oversaw the scientific library and document room, but was not invited to witness the Trinity test. Robert Serber was a member of the Manhattan District team which traveled to Japan to study the blast damage and yield of both atomic bombs. After the war, the Serbers returned to Berkeley and later moved to New York, where Robert is professor emeritus of physics at Columbia University. Charlotte Serber died in 1967.

Louis Slotin

I.D. badge photograph. Los Alamos, 1946.

Photographer: Unknown. Courtesy of LANL

Louis Slotin was a Canadian who earned his doctorate in physics at the University of Chicago. During the Manhattan Project, he was responsible for assembling the bomb's core at Trinity. After the war he became a respected leader of the Critical Assemblies Group. His was the second and last fatal criticality accident at Los Alamos during the Manhattan Project. He died at the age of thirty-five in May 1946.

Leo Szilard

Chicago, c. 1945.

Photographer: Unknown. Courtesy of the Argonne National Laboratory

Leo Szilard, the man who was almost single-handedly responsible for the inception of the Manhattan Project, was born in Hungary in 1898. Szilard studied physics in Germany, but his keen political instincts caused him to leave that country in 1933. Although he eventually settled in the United States in 1938, Szilard remained essentially rootless, often making a hotel room his home.

Szilard had the idea of a chain reaction while crossing a London road one day. He pursued this notion until he and Fermi finally began working on the experiment at Columbia University in 1939. It was Szilard who drafted the letter to President Roosevelt warning him that Germany might be making an atomic bomb.

Though Szilard was instrumental in researching and organizing the chain reaction, his involvement in the Manhattan Project was severely limited by General Groves, who did not approve of Szilard's independent mind and habits. During the war years, Szilard worked at the University of Chicago and was followed by FBI agents. After the war, he worked tirelessly to keep atomic energy under civilian control and to curb the development of atomic weapons. He was active in the Pugwash conferences in the 1950s and 60s, and founded the Council for a Livable World. He died in 1964.

Robert Wilson

On the horse he kept while living in Los Alamos, c. 1944.

Photographer: Jane Wilson. Courtesy of Robert R. Wilson

Robert Wilson, born in Wyoming in 1914, was one of the youngest group leaders at Los Alamos, where he was head of the Experimental Physics division. He was teaching at Princeton University when he was asked by Robert Oppenheimer, his former professor, to join the atomic project. After the war, Wilson refused to engage in any work which required a security clearance and later became director of Fermilab. He is currently professor emeritus of nuclear studies at Cornell University.

TIMELINE 1938–1947

1938

March
- The *Anschluss* — Germany annexes Austria and the Sudetenland.

July
- Anti-Jewish legislation is enacted in Italy.

November
- *Kristallnacht* — Nazis attack Jews and their property in Germany and Austria.
- Fermi wins Nobel Prize for physics, and leaves with his family for the United States.

December
- Otto Hahn and Fritz Strassman in Germany produce the fission of uranium.

1939

January
- Roosevelt asks Congress for 552 million dollars for defense.
- Fission is identified by Frisch, Hahn, Meitner, and Strassman.
- Niels Bohr brings the news of fission to the United States.
- Fermi and Szilard begin work on demonstrating a self-sustaining chain reaction at Columbia University.

March
- German troops complete the occupation of Czechoslovakia and stop uranium exports.
- University scientists in the United States fail to enlist the Navy's support in atomic research.

April
- Joliot-Curie demonstrates the possibility of producing a nuclear chain reaction with uranium and publishes his results.

1939

August
- Szilard, Wigner, and Teller visit Einstein to enlist his help in alerting the United States government to the possibility of Germany developing an atomic bomb, and in gaining American government support for atomic research.

September
- World War Two begins. Germany invades Poland; Britain and France declare war on Germany. The United States declares its neutrality. The U.S.S.R. invades Poland.

October
- Alexander Sachs (economist and informal advisor to the President) takes Einstein's letter to Franklin Roosevelt.
- The President's Advisory Committee on Uranium is established.

1940

February
- Dunning and Urey begin research at Columbia University on the separation of uranium-235 from natural uranium.

April
- Germany invades Norway and Denmark.
- In Britain, Otto Frisch and Rudolph Peierls calculate the theoretical critical mass of uranium needed for an atomic bomb.

May
- Germany invades Holland, Belgium, and Luxembourg.
- Churchill becomes Prime Minister of Great Britain.

1940

June
- The German Army enters Paris.
- Italy declares war on Britain and France.
- In the United States, Philip Abelson and Edwin McMillan announce the discovery of the first transuranic element, neptunium.
- The National Defense Research Council (or NDRC) is formed to coordinate university-based scientific research for military use.

July
- The Royal Air Force (or RAF) begins night bombing over Germany.
- France accepts the Japanese demand for control of Indochina.

September
- The London Blitz begins.

October
- In Japan, Hideki Tojo becomes Prime Minister of War.

November
- Franklin D. Roosevelt is elected President for a third term.

1941

January
- President Roosevelt submits a 17 billion dollar budget to Congress, which includes nearly 11 billion dollars for national defense.
- Admiral Yamamoto orders a preliminary plan for the attack of Pearl Harbor.

February
- E. McMillan, G.T. Seaborg, J.W. Kennedy, and A.C. Wahl discover a second transuranic element, later named plutonium, which shows promise of producing from nuclear fission a higher energy yield than uranium.

1941

June
- Germany invades Russia.
- The Office of Scientific Research and Development (or OSRD) and S-1 section are formed, to coordinate the development of the American atomic bomb.

July
- The British government studies the development of an atomic bomb, and issues a report, code-named MAUD.

December
- The United States expands research into the development of an atomic bomb.
- Pearl Harbor is bombed.
- The United States and Britain declare war on Japan.
- Germany and Italy declare war on the United States.
- Hong Kong surrenders to Japan.

1942

January
- Roosevelt submits a 59 billion dollar budget to Congress, including 52 billion dollars for the war effort.
- President Roosevelt and Prime Minister Churchill agree on a war strategy: the defeat of Germany first, followed by Japan.
- The Metallurgical Laboratory (or Met Lab) at the University of Chicago is established to consolidate research on a nuclear chain reaction and on plutonium.

February
- The last new automobiles are produced in the United States, as factories concentrate on making tanks and jeeps for the war.
- Atomic pile work moves to Chicago.

1942

April
- The United States interns Japanese-Americans.
- United States Forces surrender to the Japanese on the Bataan Peninsula in the Philippines. American and Philippine soldiers are forced to march to internment camps. Most die on the way. This event became known as the "Bataan Death March."

May
- Japanese troops complete their conquest of Burma.
- The Women's Auxiliary Army Corps is established.
- The 184-inch cyclotron at the University of California at Berkeley is completed.

June
- Japan loses the "Battle of the Midway."
- President Roosevelt approves a Bush and Conant proposal that the United States Army take responsibility for atomic bomb development.
- J. Robert Oppenheimer leads a group at Berkeley to investigate the theoretical aspects of making an atomic bomb and holds a conference which includes Hans Bethe, Emil Konopinski, Robert Serber, and Edward Teller. Teller raises the idea of the "super" (a thermonuclear bomb) for the first time.

August
- U.S. Marines land on Guadalcanal and the Island Campaign in the Pacific begins.
- The Manhattan Engineering District (or MED) is established. Colonel James C. Marshall is appointed District Engineer.
- The first microgram of plutonium is produced at the Met Lab.

1942

September
- Colonel Leslie Groves becomes Commander of the Manhattan Engineering District.
- Groves obtains an emergency AAA procurement rating for the Manhattan Project.
- The MED purchases 1,200 tons of uranium ore.
- Groves signs a directive authorizing the acquisition of land in eastern Tennessee upon which will be built the Clinton Engineering Works at Oak Ridge.

October
- The United States limits Anglo-American partnership in the atomic bomb program.
- Los Alamos is selected as the laboratory site to consolidate research and development for the atomic bomb.

November
- The first layer of CP-1 (Chicago pile 1) is laid under the West Stands of Stagg Field at the University of Chicago.

December
- The world's first self-sustaining nuclear chain reaction is demonstrated in Chicago.
- The Los Alamos Boys School receives notice of government intent to take over its property.
- Du Pont agrees to undertake the design, construction, and operation of plutonium production at Hanford.

1943

January
- Heavy Allied bombing of industrial centers in Germany and France begins.
- The German defeat at Stalingrad marks a turning point in the war on the Eastern Front.

February
- Construction of the Clinton Engineering Works at Oak Ridge begins.
- Construction of the Y-12 electromagnetic separation plant at Oak Ridge begins.
- Construction of the Los Alamos laboratory begins.

March
- The Special Engineer Detachment (or SED) is formed.
- Robert Oppenheimer and a few laboratory staff members arrive in Santa Fe.
- The government sends notices to local residents, requiring them to vacate the Hanford area.

April
- The University of California contract establishing the Los Alamos laboratory is formalized (and is backdated to January 1). Robert Oppenheimer is its director.
- Hans Bethe becomes the head of the Theoretical Division at Los Alamos.
- Construction of the Hanford Engineering Works begins.

May
- Captain W.S. Parsons of the Navy becomes head of the Ordnance Division at Los Alamos.
- J.W. Kennedy and C.S. Smith lead the Chemistry and Metallurgy Division at Los Alamos.

June
- Phrases such as "atomic energy," "atomic fission," and "uranium" disappear from news reports in the United States.

Heisenberg's War: The Secret History of the German Bomb (Knopf, 1994), is a dramatic investigation of Werner Heisenberg's role in the German atomic bomb effort. Two older books, one by David Irving, entitled *The German Atomic Bomb* (Simon and Schuster, 1968), and another simply titled *Alsos* (Henry Schuman, 1947) by Samuel Goudsmit, the Manhattan Project physicist who worked with the Alsos team, also bear reading. For an in-depth look at Project A, read *Project Alberta: The Preparation of Atomic Bombs for Use in World War II* by Harlow W. Russ (Exceptional Books, Los Alamos, 1984).

Two books in particular look at the Manhattan Project from the perspective of the scientists themselves: one is Robert Jungk's 1958 *Brighter than a Thousand Suns: A Personal History of the Atomic Scientists* (Harcourt Brace), and the other is Alice Kimball Smith's *A Peril and A Hope* (University of Chicago Press, 1965), which recounts the post-war scientific movement against the atomic bomb. There are also several books that focus on the decision to use atomic weapons in Hiroshima and Nagasaki, such as Martin Sherwin's *A World Destroyed: The Atomic Bomb and the Grand Alliance* (Knopf, 1975), Gar Alperovitz's *Atomic Diplomacy: Hiroshima and Potsdam* (Simon and Schuster, 1965), and Giovannitti and Freed's *The Decision to Drop the Bomb: A Political History* (Coward-McCann, 1965). For books related specifically to the damage in Hiroshima and Nagasaki, a definitive study was published in the United States in 1981 by the Committee for the Compilation of Materials on Damage Caused by the Atomic Bombs in Hiroshima and Nagasaki, entitled *Hiroshima and Nagasaki: The Physical, Medical, and Social Effects of the Atomic Bombings* (Basic Books). The United States Strategic Bombing Survey published its account of the first atomic bombings, *The Effects of the Atomic Bombs on Hiroshima and Nagasaki,* in 1946. John Hersey's original *New Yorker* article

Hiroshima, published by Knopf in 1946 as a book, is a benchmark report on the effects of the atomic bomb on several individual lives. Averill A. Liebow's *Encounter With Disaster* (W.W. Norton, 1970), and Michihiko Hachiya's *Hiroshima Diary* (University of North Carolina Press, 1955), are complementary accounts, one American, the other Japanese, of the days and weeks after the bombings. For a look at how America reacted to and has coped with the atomic bombs since 1945, read Paul Boyer's study *By the Bomb's Early Light* (Pantheon, 1985). Robert Jay Lifton has written several books and articles, including *Death in Life, Survivors of Hiroshima* (Random House, 1967), about the psychic toll the two bombs inflicted on the Japanese survivors.

There are also several books that tell the history of the two major Manhattan Project cities: Oak Ridge and Hanford. For histories of Oak Ridge, one might consult Charles W. Johnson's and Charles O. Jackson's *City Behind the Fence* (University of Tennessee Press, 1981), or *These Are Our Voices* (edited by James Overholt and published by the Children's Museum of Oak Ridge, 1987). Hanford's early history is the subject of *Hanford and the Bomb* (Living History Press, 1989) by S.L. Sanger, while Michael D'Antonio's book, *Atomic Harvest: Hanford and the Lethal Toll of America's Nuclear Arsenal* (Crown, 1993), traces its more recent past.

Personal reminiscence and memoir offer the reader yet another vantage point from which to try to comprehend what was, in essence, an extremely complex human enterprise. *Reminiscences of Los Alamos, 1943-1945* (D. Reidel, Dordrecht: Holland, 1980) edited by Lawrence Badash, is a lively collection of personal essays by several key individuals who worked on the Manhattan Project, including George Kistiakowsky, Richard Feynman, Ed and Elsie McMillan, John Manley, and Laura Fermi. Peggy Pond Church's *The House at Otowi Bridge* (University of New Mexico Press, 1960)

looks at the life of Edith Warner. Bernice Brode's 1960 essay *Tales of Los Alamos* (LASL Community News, June 2 and September 22) is perhaps the best introduction there is to what Los Alamos life was like, while Eleanor Jette's *Inside Box 1663* (Los Alamos Historical Society, 1977), offers another personal reminiscence. These efforts are amplified by the essays in *Standing By and Making Do* (Los Alamos Historical Society, 1988), written by nine women who lived in the secret city, and *All in Our Time* (edited by Jane Wilson, and published by the Bulletin of the Atomic Scientists, 1975), which contains an interesting series of essays by Manhattan Project scientists. Laura Fermi's engagingly written 1954 memoir, *Atoms in the Family* (University of Chicago Press, 1954), describes the Fermis' experience as new American emigrants and provides a well written introduction to atomic theory. Leona Marshall Libby's *The Uranium People* (Crane, Russak & Company, Inc. Charles Scribner's and Sons, 1979), is an idiosyncratic account of the Manhattan Project from one of the few female physicists on the Project.

The field of autobiography and biography relating to the Manhattan Project is growing ever larger. For those interested in some of the great scientific minds who worked on the atomic bomb, there are several books by and about Robert Oppenheimer, the director and guiding spirit of the Los Alamos laboratory — including Peter Goodchild's *Oppenheimer: Shatterer of Worlds* (Fromm International, 1985), and Nuel P. Davis's *Lawrence and Oppenheimer* (Simon and Schuster, 1968), about the relationship between Oppenheimer and the inventor of the cyclotron. There are also several volumes containing Oppenheimer's eloquent essays and addresses, including *Atom and Void: Essays on Science and Community* (Princeton University Press, 1989), *Uncommon Sense* (Birkhauser Boston, 1984), and *Robert Oppenheimer: Letters and Recollections* (Harvard University Press, 1980), edited by Charles Weiner and Alice Kimball Smith.

1943

June
- Construction of X-10, the Oak Ridge pilot nuclear reactor, begins.
- Construction of K-25, the Oak Ridge gaseous diffusion plant, begins.
- A delivery program (part of the Ordnance Division), led by N.F. Ramsey, is initiated at Los Alamos.
- A survey of planes suitable to carry and deliver the atomic bombs is made. The B-29 is selected.
- The construction of nuclear reactors at Hanford begins.

July
- The Allies land in Italy.
- R.F. Bacher leads the Experimental Physics Division at Los Alamos.
- The first implosion experiments are performed at Los Alamos.

August
- The Quebec Agreement is signed by Britain and the United States, governing the collaboration of the British and American atomic bomb projects.

September
- Italy surrenders to the Allies.

November
- The X-10 nuclear reactor at Oak Ridge goes critical.

December
- General Eisenhower is named commander of Allied Forces in Europe.
- A special U.S. foreign intelligence mission in Europe is established and code-named Alsos.
- The first members of the British Mission arrive in Los Alamos.

1944

January
- The RAF bombs Berlin with 2,300 tons of explosives.
- The siege of Leningrad is lifted.
- The Y-12 plant at Oak Ridge is fully operational.

February
- The first sample of enriched uranium from Y-12 arrives in Los Alamos.

March
- A decision is made at Los Alamos to test the implosion design of the atomic bomb.
- The first tests of ballistic shapes and fusing equipment begins at Muroc, California.

April
- The first sample of plutonium from the Oak Ridge X-10 reactor arrives in Los Alamos.

May
- The Hanford Engineering Works construction force peaks at 45,000 workers.

June
- The D-Day landings in Normandy, France, commence.
- First U.S. B-29 attack of Japanese targets occurs at Bangkok.
- First U.S. "strategic" bombing raids of Japan.
- The United States launches a campaign for the Marianas Islands in the Pacific.
- The MED employs 129,000 people: 84,500 in construction; 40,500 operating staff; 1,800 military personnel; and 1,800 in the Civil Service.
- The construction of the first plutonium producing reactor is completed at Hanford.

July

- Saipan surrenders to the United States.
- The invasion of Tinian begins.
- The construction of S-50, the thermal diffusion plant at Oak Ridge, begins.
- Spontaneous fission is discovered in plutonium.
- The gun-assembly design for the plutonium weapon is rejected.

August

- Paris is liberated.
- Tinian and Guam are captured by the United States. The Marianas Islands are selected as bases from which the American Forces will advance on Japan.
- Alsos reaches Paris.
- The Los Alamos laboratory is reorganized to concentrate on the implosion method for the plutonium bomb. Three new divisions are formed: Weapons and Physics, led by Bacher; Explosives, led by Kistiakowsky; and F Division (to look at various nuclear physics problems, including the "super") led by Fermi. Theoretical Physics and the Chemistry and Metallurgy Divisions are unchanged. The Experimental Physics Division, renamed Research, is now led by Robert Wilson, and the Ordnance Division is led by Captain W.S. Parsons.

September

- Brussels is liberated.
- The Jornada del Muerto, near Alamogordo, New Mexico is selected as the Trinity test site.
- The 509th Composite Group arrives at Wendover Field, Utah.
- The two basic bomb designs — Fat Man and Little Boy — are finalized.
- The first Hanford plutonium producing reactor goes critical.

October

- The United States invades the Philippines.
- German troops evacuate Athens.
- Soviet troops enter East Prussia.
- The United States achieves victory in the Battle of Leyte Gulf, despite first Kamikaze attacks by the Japanese.
- Fifteen modified B-29's arrive at Wendover Field, Utah, where drop testing of bomb shapes begins.

November

- President Roosevelt is re-elected for an unprecedented fourth consecutive term.
- Air raids on Tokyo begin from Saipan.
- Alsos reaches Strasbourg, where documents reveal no serious German atomic bomb project.

December

- U.S. Third Army ends siege of Bastogne, known as the "Battle of the Bulge."
- Base camp at Trinity site is completed.
- The first chemical separation plant at Hanford becomes operational.
- The second Hanford plutonium producing reactor goes critical.

January

- Soviet troops liberate Auschwitz.
- U.S. Forces land in Luzon in the Philippines.

February

- American bombers raid Berlin, where the firestorms kill an estimated 135,000 people.
- Bataan is recaptured by U.S. Forces.
- U.S. Marines land on Iwo Jima.
- Preparations for Project Alberta's overseas base on Tinian begin.

1945

February

- The first 100 grams of liquid plutonium nitrate are sent from Hanford to Los Alamos.
- The third Hanford plutonium producing reactor goes critical. The second chemical separation plant is completed.
- The Hanford construction camp is closed.
- Dresden is fire-bombed by the British and American Air Forces.

March

- The United States fire-bombs Tokyo, where a firestorm kills an estimated 124,000 people in a single night.
- Project Alberta (combat use of the atomic bomb) officially begins; it is led by Captain W. S. Parsons.
- Physicist Kenneth Bainbridge is appointed director of the Trinity test.
- S-50 becomes operational at Oak Ridge.
- Regular weekly shipments of uranium-235 are sent to Los Alamos (enough material will have been produced by July for the Little Boy bomb, and by mid-November for a second gun-assembly device).
- Full-scale production at Hanford begins (266 pounds of plutonium is produced by the end of 1945, sufficient for nineteen Fat Man units).

April

- Buchenwald and Dachau concentration camps are liberated by American troops.
- President Roosevelt dies. Vice-President Truman becomes President.
- Truman first learns about the Manhattan Project.
- U.S. Forces land on Okinawa.
- Benito Mussolini is executed.
- German Forces in Italy surrender.
- Hitler commits suicide.
- Alsos dismantles the only German reactor it finds.
- The construction of special bomb assembly facilities begins on Tinian.

1945

May

- Germany surrenders. Victory-in-Europe-Day is May 8.
- The Interim Committee meets in Washington, D.C., to discuss wartime and post-war uses of the atomic bomb and atomic energy.
- The United Nations is organized.
- U.S. Joint Chiefs of Staff approve an invasion of Japan for November.
- The 100-ton TNT test is held at Trinity site.
- The total number of personnel at Los Alamos is 2,231. The average age of the scientific staff is twenty-nine.

June

- Japanese Premier Suzuki declares Japan will not unconditionally surrender.
- U.S. Forces capture Okinawa.
- The Interim Committee recommends that the atomic bombs be dropped without prior warning.
- General Douglas MacArthur first learns of the atomic bomb.
- The 509th and Project Alberta scientific members begin arriving on Tinian.

July 14

- Little Boy leaves Los Alamos for Tinian.

July 16

- The first atomic explosion occurs at 05:29:45 Mountain War Time in the New Mexican desert.
- President Truman, at Potsdam, learns that the Trinity test is successful.

July 17

- Chicago scientists from the Met Lab address a petition to the President, asking for a demonstration of the atomic bomb before a military strike.
- Potsdam conference begins.

1945

July 24
- The Potsdam Declaration demands the unconditional surrender of Japan.
- President Truman decides to use the atomic bomb, and mentions to Stalin that the United States possesses a powerful new weapon.
- Nagasaki is added to the target list.
- Pumpkin missions begin over Japan to accustom the enemy to small, high-altitude, unescorted B-29 flights.

July 28
- Japan rejects the demands of the Potsdam Declaration.
- All Fat Man components arrive at Tinian.

August 6
- The first atomic bomb (Little Boy) is dropped on Hiroshima.

August 8
- The U.S.S.R. declares war on Japan.

August 9
- The second atomic bomb (Fat Man) is dropped on Nagasaki.

August 10
- Japan sues for peace.
- President Truman orders the cessation of atomic bombings.

August 12
- General Groves telephones Los Alamos to halt shipment of a second active plutonium core.
- The Smyth Report (a public account of the development of the atomic bomb) is released to the public.

August 14
- World War Two ends. During the war an estimated 54.8 million people, in fifty-seven nations, mostly civilians, died. Ten million people are displaced.

1945

August 21
- Critical assembly accident occurs at Los Alamos. Harry Daghlian receives a fatal dose of radiation and dies three weeks later.

August 28
- The United States Occupation Forces land in Japan.

September
- Formal surrender of Japan is signed on board the *U.S.S. Missouri* in Tokyo Bay.
- Japanese Forces in China surrender.
- The Manhattan Project Atomic Bomb Investigating Team arrives in Japan.
- The British Mission hold a farewell party at Los Alamos.

October
- The May-Johnson Bill advocating military control of atomic weapons research is presented to Congress.
- Robert Oppenheimer resigns as director of the Los Alamos laboratory. Norris E. Bradbury succeeds him.

December
- The McMahon Bill, advocating civilian control of atomic energy and weapons research is presented to Congress.
- Operation Crossroads is proposed: the Navy requests that the Los Alamos laboratory direct the technical aspects of the test, which will observe the effects of a nuclear weapon on naval vessels.
- Oak Ridge's population is 42,700.
- Many Los Alamos scientists, including L. Alvarez, E. Fermi, G. Kistiakowsky, G. Seaborg, E. Segrè, and V. Weisskopf leave the laboratory to return to their university posts.
- The population of Richland, at Hanford, is 15,000.

1946

January
- The first session of the United Nations is held in London.

March
- Churchill delivers his "Iron Curtain" speech in Fulton, Missouri, marking the symbolic beginning of the Cold War.

April
- A conference is held at Los Alamos to discuss the feasibility of a thermonuclear bomb (the "super").

May
- Second critical assembly accident occurs at Los Alamos. Louis Slotin receives a fatal dose of radiation and dies nine days later.

June
- The United States nuclear stockpile consists of nine Fat Man bombs (only seven are operational).
- The Baruch Plan for international control of nuclear weapons is presented to the United Nations: all nations would agree not to produce atomic bombs; an international agency would conduct inspections, and the United States would cede its atomic arsenal to the agency. The plan is rejected by the U.S.S.R.
- Operation Crossroads, Able test. The U.S. Navy explodes an atomic bomb in the air above a fleet of vessels near the Bikini atoll.

July
- A Soviet proposal for the international control of nuclear weapons is presented to the United Nations by Andrei Gromyko: the United States would destroy its nuclear arsenal before the creation of an international agency. The plan is rejected by the U.S.

1946

- Operation Crossroads, Baker test. The U.S. Navy explodes an atomic bomb in shallow water below a fleet of navy vessels.
- The "Bikini" swimsuit is modeled at a Paris fashion show.

August
- President Truman signs the Atomic Energy Act, which creates a five-person civilian commission to control the development of atomic energy in the United States. David Lilienthal is appointed its first commissioner.
- The first shipment of radioisotopes for cancer research leaves Oak Ridge.

September
- The Nuremberg war crimes trials are held in Germany.
- The first United States patent for a nuclear fusion bomb is filed by Teller, Oppenheimer, Konopinski, and Bethe.

1947

January
- The Atomic Energy Commission is formed and takes over responsibility for atomic energy and nuclear weapons. The Manhattan Engineering District officially ends January 1.

Page from photo album. Los Alamos, February 1944.

Photographer: Jean Critchfield.
Courtesy of Jean Critchfield

GLOSSARY

ALPHA PARTICLE (ALPHA RAY)

A sub-atomic particle identical to the nucleus of a helium atom, that is, two protons and two neutrons. It is one of the products of spontaneous nuclear disintegration of radioactive elements such as radium. Alpha particles readily interact with matter and so have only a short range: they can travel only a few centimeters in air.

ATOM

From the Greek, *atomos,* meaning "that which cannot be cut up." It is the unit of matter that cannot be broken down chemically into anything simpler. An atom consists of a central nucleus, composed of positively charged protons and chargeless neutrons, surrounded by negatively charged electrons equal in number to the protons in the nucleus so that the net charge on the atom is zero.
Atomic number: the number of protons in the atomic nucleus.
Atomic mass number: the total number of protons and neutrons in the atomic nucleus.
Ion: an atom which has either gained or lost one or more electrons, leaving it negatively or positively charged.

ATOMIC BOMB (A-BOMB)

A bomb employing a supercritical fission chain reaction to produce its explosive energy.

ATOMIC PILE

Original term for a nuclear reactor.

BALLISTICS

The study of projectiles moving under the force of gravity.

BETA PARTICLE (BETA RAY)

An electron. The term is generally used for electrons that arise from radioactive decay, such as those emitted by radioactive isotope phosphorous-32. Electrons do not exist as such in the atomic nucleus: beta particles are produced by the conversion of neutrons into protons. Beta rays (streams of beta particles) are more penetrating than alpha particles but less penetrating than gamma rays.

CALUTRON

A contraction of CALifornia University CycloTRON. An apparatus built by E.O. Lawrence for the separation of the isotopes uranium-235 and uranium-238, based on a mass spectrometer and cyclotron. The uranium is ionized, and the positively charged ions accelerated to high velocities into a field where a powerful magnet deflects them into semicircular paths. The curve of the path differs according to the mass of the ion (ions of uranium-235 are deflected more than the heavier ions of uranium-238), so that the ions can be collected separately.

CAPTURE

Process by which an atom acquires an additional particle, for example, a neutron.

CHAIN REACTION

A self-sustaining process in which the products of the initial event go on to produce similar events. In a nuclear fission chain reaction, an atomic nucleus is split by a neutron, thereby releasing further neutrons, which then split other nuclei and release yet more neutrons. A self-sustaining chain reaction can only occur when the number of neutrons released continues to equal or outnumber those that are lost (through leakage, absorption by impurities, etc.). In the case of an atomic bomb, the chain reaction is uncontrolled and escalates into a massive explosion. In the case of a nuclear reactor, the chain reaction is controlled and maintained at a set level.

CONTROL ROD

A rod or bar made of a substance that strongly absorbs neutrons, which is inserted into a nuclear reactor to regulate the chain reaction. Control rods absorb neutrons so that the chain reaction is slowed or stopped as the rods enter the reactor.

CRITICAL MASS

The minimum amount of fissile material required to sustain a nuclear chain reaction. A supercritical mass is one that exceeds the critical mass and can therefore lead to the escalating chain reaction necessary for an atomic explosion. A subcritical mass is one in which a chain reaction is not maintained.

CYCLOTRON

A mechanism invented in 1931 by E.O. Lawrence for the bombardment of atomic nuclei by highly accelerated, positively-charged particles in order to produce transmutations and artificial radioactivity. Two semicircular electrodes are contained in a vacuum chamber in between the poles of a large electromagnet. An alternating electric field between the electrodes accelerates the sub-atomic particles, which are made to travel in spiral paths in the magnetic field, until a deflector hurls them against the nuclei of target atoms.

DECAY (RADIOACTIVE)

The gradual diminishing of a radioactive substance due to the spontaneous disintegration of its atomic nuclei, usually by emission of particles or by fission.

ELECTRON

A stable elementary particle with a negative charge of one unit and a mass about 1/1800 of that of a proton or neutron. The charge on the electron is the basic unit of charge: all electric charges are multiples of the electron charge.

ELEMENT

A substance consisting only of atoms with the same atomic number but not necessarily the same atomic mass number (see isotope). There are ninety-two naturally occurring elements.

ENRICHMENT

The process of increasing the proportion of a particular isotope of an element to a level greater than its natural abundance.

FALLOUT

Radioactive material released into the air or deposited on the earth's surface as the result of a nuclear explosion. Fallout particles vary greatly in size, degree of radioactivity, and distribution over an affected area. The nature and effects of fallout are influenced by such variables as the weather, height of the blast from the earth's surface, type of material caught up in the explosion, and the configuration of the terrain over which the blast occurs.

FISSILE MATERIAL

Material containing isotopes of elements that can undergo nuclear fission and produce a fission chain reaction. Uranium-235 and plutonium are examples of fissile material.

FISSION (NUCLEAR)

Nuclear fission is the splitting of an atomic nucleus into two or more major fragments. This may occur spontaneously in the heaviest elements, or may be induced by the bombardment of fissile material with neutrons. The process has been likened to a liquid drop being stretched until it breaks into two smaller droplets. The smaller nuclei produced are called fission by-products and vary in size.

FOGGING

A photographic term used to define any visible deposit or density in a negative or print that does not result from the photographic image itself.

FIZZLE

A non-technical term used to describe an atomic bomb that does not reach the supercritical mass required for an explosion, but which may release some energy by fission at a subcritical mass level.

FUSION

A nuclear reaction in which light nuclei combine to form a nucleus of a higher mass number, with the release of energy. Fusion may be viewed as the inverse of fission, but energy is released only when very light elements undergo fusion or very heavy elements undergo fission. A single fusion reaction releases more energy than a single fission reaction. Fusion is the energy-releasing process in stars, including our sun. At present, man-made fusion reactions cannot be controlled and can be utilized only for bombs (cf. hydrogen bomb), whereas fission reactions can be controlled in nuclear reactors and used for power production as well as for bombs.

GAMMA RAYS (GAMMA RADIATION)

Electromagnetic radiation of very short wavelength; that is, photons of high energy. Unlike alpha and beta rays, gamma rays are highly penetrating. Their penetrating power depends on their wavelength, which in turn depends on the nuclear reaction from which they derive. Low frequency (soft) gamma rays penetrate about half an inch of lead, while high frequency (hard) gamma rays may penetrate several inches of lead. Gamma rays can readily penetrate living tissue and damage it. They can destroy cells and in humans cause genetic mutations, sterility, burns, and, at high dosage, death. However, the cell-destroying capacity of gamma rays are used in nuclear medicine for both treatment and diagnosis.

HALF-LIFE

The period of time in which the radioactivity of a substance drops to one-half of its initial value, i.e., the time it takes for one-half the atoms of the substance to decay. The half-life value of any one isotope is independent of temperature, pressure or chemical state, but varies between isotopes from less than a millionth of a second to more than a million years.

HYDROGEN BOMB (H-BOMB, THERMO-NUCLEAR BOMB, THE "SUPER")

A bomb employing the principle of nuclear fusion. A hydrogen bomb's yield is usually in the megaton range.

IMPLOSION

An explosion focused inwards. The plutonium bomb dropped on Nagasaki utilized the implosion process to achieve a supercritical mass of plutonium.

INITIATOR

A neutron source employed to start a fast nuclear chain reaction in an implosion bomb. The initiator used to detonate the first plutonium bomb, called the "urchin" (designed by a group led by Charles Critchfield), was developed at Los Alamos. It was made of beryllium and polonium (which when mixed are strong neutron emitters) and, when placed between the two subcritical hemispheres of plutonium, would, at the moment of implosion, mix together causing the sudden initiation of a violent chain reaction in the supercritical mass of plutonium.

IONIZATION

The process of forming ions, whereby an atom or molecule gains or loses an electron, thus acquiring a net electrical charge.

ISOTOPE

Isotopes are atoms of the same element, which all have the same atomic mass number or atomic weight as well as the same atomic number. An element may contain more than one isotope; nearly all elements found in nature are made up of several. Isotopes of a given element are chemically indistinguishable.

MASS SPECTROMETER

A device used to separate isotopes by weight and to detect them electrically. It was later adapted by Alfred O. Nier to find leaks in the airtight gaseous-diffusion plant at Oak Ridge. A mass spectrograph is a similar device but utilizes photographic means of detection.

METALLURGY

The science and technology of metals, which includes their extraction, alloying, and hardening.

MODERATOR

A material used to reduce the speed of fast neutrons produced by nuclear fission. Neutrons slowed down by collision with the nuclei of a moderator are much more likely to cause the fission of fissile material than are fast neutrons. The first nuclear reactors at Chicago, Argonne, and Hanford employed pure graphite as their moderator.

NEPTUNIUM

A highly unstable, radioactive element produced artificially. It was identified as the first transuranic element in 1940 by E.M. McMillan and P. Abelson at the University of California, Berkeley. Neptunium is an intermediate product in the production of plutonium from uranium. It was named after Neptune, the planet beyond Uranus.

NEUTRON

An elementary particle that is electrically neutral, and has a slightly greater mass than that of the proton. Neutrons are found in all atomic nuclei except that of hydrogen.

Fast neutrons: neutrons emitted by nuclear fission, not slowed by collision.

Slow neutrons: neutrons which have lost most of their energy due to a series of impacts with a moderator.

NUCLEAR ENERGY

The energy released from the nucleus of an atom in any kind of nuclear reaction (fission, fusion, beta decay, etc.).

NUCLEAR REACTOR

An apparatus designed and operated to generate nuclear energy that is converted into heat for power purposes. It can also be used for the production of plutonium or radioisotopes for research and medicine. At present, all reactors work on the nuclear fission chain reaction principle: fissile material is mixed with a moderator and regulated by control rods. Reactors may be described in terms of their function, their moderator, or their coolant.

NUCLEUS (ATOMIC)

The positively charged central part of an atom which constitutes nearly all its mass. It is composed of one or more protons and, with the exception of hydrogen, one or more neutrons.

PINHOLE CAMERA

A photographic camera which forms an image on film by means of a very small hole instead of a lens.

PLUTONIUM

An artificially produced radioactive element. First produced by G.T. Seaborg, E.M. McMillan, J.W. Kennedy, and A.C. Wahl at the University of California, Berkeley, in 1940, plutonium was named for the planet Pluto. It is one of the most toxic substances known, but is not particularly radioactive, with a half-life of 24,400 years.

Plutonium-239, the important fissile isotope, was produced shortly after by J.W. Kennedy, E. Segrè, A.C. Wahl, and E.M. McMillan. This isotope was used in the Fat Man bomb dropped on Nagasaki.

RADIOACTIVITY (RADIATION)

The spontaneous transmutation of unstable isotopes (called radioactive isotopes), accompanied by the emission of radiation in the form of alpha, beta, or gamma rays, and/or neutrons. Some radioactive isotopes occur in nature (natural radioactivity), but artificial radioactive isotopes of most elements can be produced by bombardment with particles (e.g., neutrons).

Ionizing radiation: radiation that causes ionization of atoms during its passage through matter. Alpha and beta rays have greater ionizing effects than do gamma rays or neutrons. Most of the damage that radiation causes to living tissue occurs through ionization.

RADIATION SICKNESS

Illness resulting from exposure to radiation. The term is usually restricted to generalized illness, as opposed to local radiation burns or to genetic damage, which appears only as mutations in progeny. Symptoms are both gastrointestinal and neurologic.

RADIOCHEMISTRY

The chemical study of radioactive isotopes and isotopes produced by nuclear reactions, required for identifying or purifying the products of nuclear reactions.

RADIOISOTOPE

A radioactive isotope, either naturally occurring or artificially produced. Radioactive isotopes are used in medicine as tracers for diagnosis and as radiation sources for the treatment of tumors.

SLUGS

Fuel for the first nuclear reactors at Hanford consisting of pieces of metallic uranium, encased in solder to prevent corrosion, which were arranged in a lattice-like structure within blocks of graphite.

SOLARIZATION

The reversal of the image on film by extreme over-exposure to light.

TAMPER

In an atomic bomb, an interior metallic coating intended to reflect neutrons into the interior of the bomb and so reduce their leakage. Also called a reflector.

TRANSMUTATION

The change of one element into another. Once the aim of alchemy, transmutation was subsequently thought to be impossible (before the advent of nuclear physics): it is now known to occur naturally in radioactive elements and can be induced artificially in nuclear reactors and other devices.

TRANSURANIC ELEMENTS

Elements with atomic numbers higher than 92, that of uranium. These elements, which are not found in nature, are produced artificially by various nuclear processes.

TRINITITE

The artificial mineral produced by the Trinity explosion at Alamogordo, New Mexico, on July 16, 1945. It appeared as a thin, green layer of glassy fused earth. Many pieces were collected as souvenirs and made into jewelry. Though not intensely radioactive, the mineral could cause radiation burns if worn next to the skin.

URANIUM

The heaviest naturally occurring element (atomic number 92); all of its isotopes are radioactive. Uranium was discovered in 1789 by M.H. Klaproth and its name derives from the then recently discovered planet Uranus. The isotope uranium-235 is fissionable but only makes up approximately 0.7 percent of naturally-occurring uranium.

YIELD

The explosive power of a nuclear weapon, usually measured as the amount of TNT (a conventional chemical explosive) that would be required to produce the same energy. The yield of a fission bomb is in the range of kilotons of TNT (1 kiloton = 1,000 tons of TNT); that of a fusion bomb is in the range of megatons (1 megaton = 1 million tons of TNT).

ZERO (GROUND ZERO, POINT ZERO, HYPOCENTER, EPICENTER)

The point on the ground under a nuclear explosion.

ANNOTATED BIBLIOGRAPHY

Several general histories about the Manhattan District have been written, some more technical than others. Richard Rhodes's 1986 book, ***The Making of the Atomic Bomb*** (Simon and Schuster) is a masterly and compelling account not only of how the atomic bomb was made, but of the great scientific discoveries and political climate that made such an invention possible. Richard G. Hewlett's and Oscar E. Anderson's official three-volume history of the Atomic Energy Commission, of which the first volume (1939–1946), ***The New World*** (University of California Press, 1990) is concerned with the Manhattan District, looks at the interrelationship between the military and scientific communities and how each contributed to the making of the bomb. For a comprehensive scientific account of the Los Alamos contribution, consult David Hawkins's, Edith C. Truslow's and Ralph Carlisle Smith's ***Manhattan District History, Project Y: The Los Alamos Story*** (Tomash Publishers, 1983), or the 1993 book ***Critical Assembly: A Technical History of Los Alamos during the Oppenheimer Years, 1943-1945,*** by Lillian Hoddeson, Paul W. Henriksen, Roger A. Meade, and Catherine Westfall (Cambridge University Press). Vincent C. Jones's ***Manhattan: The Army and the Atomic Bomb*** (published by the U.S. Army Center of Military History, Washington, D.C., in 1985) is part of the Army Historical Series on World War II. It is primarily a technical history of the Manhattan Project, but also gives a good idea of how the Army Corps of Engineers directed the secret effort. Anthony Cave Brown's and Charles B. MacDonald's ***The Secret History of the Atomic Bomb*** (Delta, 1977) is an edited version of the originally classified history of the Manhattan District now housed at the National Archives in Washington, D.C. It also contains the hard-to-find original Smyth Report, which was written and published for the general public, amid some controversy, in August 1945. Michael Stoff's ***The Manhattan Project: A Documentary Introduction to the Atomic Age*** (Temple University Press, 1991) also uses original documents to provide an inside look at how the Project was organized. For a popular book which reveals the mind-boggling contribution of industry, Stephane Groueff's ***Manhattan Project: The Untold Story of the Atomic Bomb*** (Little, Brown, 1977) relates how the army involved many industrial giants in mid-century America to work on the atomic bomb. ***Dawn Over Zero*** (Knopf, 1946) is an account of the Manhattan Project written by William Laurence, the *New York Times* journalist who was the only reporter aware of the top-secret project, while Leslie Groves's 1962 memoir ***Now It Can Be Told*** (Harper & Row) gives the reader a detailed look at how the general organized the many components of the Manhattan District.

There are also books which deal with particular aspects of the Manhattan Project. Ferenc Szasz's ***The Day the Sun Rose Twice*** (University of New Mexico Press, 1984), and Lansing Lamont's ***Day of Trinity*** (Atheneum, 1965), describe the great effort that went into the detonation of the world's first atomic bomb near Alamogordo, New Mexico. James Kunetka's ***City of Fire: Los Alamos and the Birth of the Atomic Age 1943-1945*** (Prentice Hall, 1978) recounts the story of the Manhattan Project from the perspective of Los Alamos. For a history of the British involvement, see Ferenc Szasz's ***British Scientists and the Manhattan Project: The Los Alamos Years*** (St. Martins Press, 1992), and Margaret Gowing's ***Britain and Atomic Energy 1939–1945*** (Macmillan, 1964). The health aspects of the Manhattan Project are detailed in Barton Hacker's ***The Dragon's Tail: Radiation Safety During the Manhattan Project 1942–1946*** (University of California Press, 1987), and ***Health Physics: A Backward Glance*** (Pergamon Press, 1980), edited by Ronald L. Kathren and Paul L. Ziemer. For those who would like to read more about the Alsos spy mission, Thomas Powers's

For more insight about the driven Hungarian scientist Leo Szilard, look at **Leo Szilard: His Version of the Facts** (MIT Press, 1978), edited by Spencer R. Weart and Gertrud Weiss Szilard, and the biography written by William Lanouette, **Genius in the Shadows: A Biography of Leo Szilard: The Man Behind the Bomb** (Scribner's 1993). Jeremy Bernstein's profile of Hans Bethe, the leader of the Theoretical Division at Los Alamos was published as **Hans Bethe, Prophet of Energy** (Basic Books, 1980), while Bethe's own autobiography is entitled **Road from Los Alamos** (Simon and Schuster, 1991). Richard Feynman, who was only twenty-five when he arrived in Los Alamos, wrote several books. His **Surely You're Joking Mr. Feynman** (W.W. Norton, 1985) contains a very readable memoir of Los Alamos. Feynman is also the subject of James Gleick's 1992 **Genius** (Pantheon), which charts the fascinating career of the scientific iconoclast. Other scientific biographies and autobiographies include Victor Weisskopf's 1991 **The Joy of Insight** (Basic Books), Emilio Segrè's **A Mind Always in Motion** (University of California Press, 1993), Segrè's 1970 biography entitled **Enrico Fermi, Physicist** (University of Chicago Press), Stanislaw Ulam's **Adventures of a Mathematician** (Scribner's, 1976), and Otto Frisch's **What Little I Remember** (Cambridge University Press, 1979).

Several biographies and autobiographies of some of the important but lesser known figures of the Manhattan Project are available. These include: Vannevar Bush's **Modern Arms and Free Men** (Simon and Schuster, 1949), Arthur Holly Compton's **Atomic Quest** (Oxford University Press, 1956), and **The Cosmos of Arthur Holly Compton** (Knopf, 1967), as well as the 1993 biography of James Conant by James G. Hershberg entitled, **James B. Conant: Harvard to Hiroshima and the Making of the Nuclear Age** (Knopf, 1993).

Finally, several books of photography on nuclear themes relate to the Manhattan Project in terms of general subject matter. Robert del Tredici's **At Work in the Fields of the Bomb** (Harper and Row, 1987), looks at nuclear power facilities and includes an interview with Berlyn Brixner. Carole Gallagher's **American Ground Zero** (MIT Press, 1993), is a photographic and textual documentation of the downwinders and military personnel who have been affected by atomic testing. Robert Adams, David Graham, Peter Goin, David Hansen, Richard Misrach, Patrick Nagatani, John Pfahl, and Meridel Rubenstein are all contemporary photographers who have photographed nuclear power plants and nuclear landscapes.

ACKNOWLEDGMENTS

This book was not only a collaboration between its two authors, but between them and the many people whose images are reflected on its pages. Three people in particular should be mentioned: Nella Fermi Weiner, who throughout gave us support and encouragement, and whose photographs initially prompted the project; Richard Rhodes, who encouraged us and whose book, *The Making of the Atomic Bomb*, introduced and eloquently guided us through the complex world of the Manhattan Project; and Roger Meade, archivist at the Los Alamos National Laboratory, who, for more than four years, has dealt with an endless number of requests and visits with both good grace and good humor.

Robert Serber, Berlyn Brixner, and Richard Garwin gave us valuable and meticulous assistance with scientific, technical, photographic, and historical details.

We have been fortunate enough to have corresponded with and met many of the individuals and their families who participated in the work of the Manhattan Engineering District. Their generosity, insight, and enthusiasm for this project have been very significant to both of us. Thank you to Jack Aeby, Beverly and Harold Agnew, Kenneth T. Bainbridge, Henry and Shirley Barnett, Heinz Barschall, Hans and Rosa Bethe, Jim Coon, Jean Critchfield, Carl Crumb, Jean Dabney, Anne Denman, George Farwell, Anthony and Naomi French, Robert Furman, Murph and Mildred Goldberger, Crawford Greenewalt, David Hawkins, Burton Helberg, Joan Hinton, Robley Johnson, Bill Jones, Don and Dorothy Kerst, L.D.P. King, Morris Kolodney, Jerrold Lewis, Gordon Linder, Mary Mack, H.G. MacPherson, Kay Manley, John Marshall Jr., John Marshall III, Nick Metropolis, Mike Michnovicz, Al Milch, Philip Moon, Philip Morrison, Edward Onstott, Rudolf Peierls, Andy and Mary Neddermeyer, Peter Oppenheimer, Hugh T. Richards, Frank Shelton, Alice Kimball Smith, Stewart Smith, Harlow W. Russ, Rosa and Claudio Segrè, Pat and Ruby Sherr, Edward and Mici Teller, Françoise Ulam, Fausta Walsby, Al Wattenberg, Richard Watts, Victor Weisskopf, Ed and Esther Westcott, John Wheeler, and Robert and Jane Wilson.

We had help collecting photographs of the 509th Composite Group from Russell Gackenbach, Robert Krauss, Charles Levy, and Fred Olivi.

Many others helped us with our photographic, scientific, and historical research at the Manhattan Project's three major sites. In New Mexico, we would like to thank J. Arthur Freed, Don Peterson, Fred Rick, Bill Jack Rodgers, Molly Rodriguez, Linda Sandoval, and Robert Seidel at the Los Alamos National Laboratory; Teresa Strottman and Rebecca Collinsworth at the Los Alamos Historical Society; Joni Hezlep and Rick Ray at the National Atomic Museum in Albuquerque. In Tennessee, Alvin Weinberg, Jim Alexander, Ruth Carey, Waldo E. Cohn, Paul Frame, and Frank Hoffman at the Oak Ridge National Laboratory facilitated our work. Patricia Bernard-Ezzell from the Tennessee Valley Authority, the reference staffs of the University of Tennessee Special Collections Department, and the Oak Ridge Public Library helped us locate historical photographs. In Washington State at Hanford, Jay Haney of the Westinghouse Hanford Company generously shared his knowledge of Hanford's history and gave us considerable help in locating photographs. Ron Kathren, from Washington State University, devoted much time assisting us in our search for health physics material.

We consulted various archives, both public and private throughout the country. In Illinois, we would like to thank Pat Canaday at the Argonne National Laboratory, and Richard Popp at the Joseph Regenstein Library of the University of Chicago. In Washington, D.C., Nick Natanson at the National Archives, Still Picture Branch, deserves a special thank you. We also thank Edwin Reis at the Military Research Branch at the

National Archives; Spencer Weart and Tracy Kieffer from the American Institute of Physics; Martin Gordon at the Army Corps of Engineers, Office of History; Mike Rhode at the Armed Forces Institute of Pathology; and Leonard Bruno at the Library of Congress. In New York, we had help from Bernard Crystal, Rhea Pliakas, and Holly Haswell at Columbia University and the University Archives, Fred Knuble at the Columbia University public information office; Christopher Hoolihan at the Edward G. Miner Library at the University of Rochester; Janet Sellis at the Brookhaven National Laboratory; Betty Hallenstein at the G.E. Hall of History, and the reference desk staffs at the White Plains and Greenburgh Public Libraries. At other MED sites in the United States, we would like to thank Frank Cook at the University Archives, University of Wisconsin; Beverly Freeman at the Decatur Public Library; Betty Erickson and Tyler Walters at the University Archives/Iowa State University; Dianne Borgen at the Ames Laboratory; Judith Simonsen at the Milwaukee County Historical Society; Ed Lofghren, Rita McClean, Mary Padilla, and David Yan from the Lawrence Berkeley Laboratory; and the archivists at the Hagley Museum and Library in Delaware and the University of Pennsylvania Archives and the Moore School of Engineering.

We have benefited from contact with numerous colleagues, among them historians, scientists, writers, and photographers. Many thanks to Agnes Arnao, Laura Benkov, Rick Bolton, Gus Bosco, Paul Boyer, Jim Chimbidis, Robert del Tredici, Jon Else, Lila and Ugo Fano, Lorraine Ferguson, Kenneth Ford, Carole Gallagher, James Gleick, Stanley Goldberg, Barton Hacker, Diane Karp and New Observations, Bob Kaczorowski and Camden County College, Linda Klingler, Adrienne Kolb, William Lanouette, Riccardo Levi-Setti, Priscilla McMillan, Greg Mitchell, Carole Naggar, Jay Orear, Jack Pesda, Thomas Powers, Fred Ritchin, Meridel Rubenstein, Jay Ruby, Robert Sachs, Steve Sanger, Lynn Silverman, Newell Stannard, Ferenc Szasz, Nan Talese, Linda and Jack Viertel, Helaine Wasser, Adam Weinberg, and Stanley Weintraub. We would also like to thank Paul Gottlieb at Harry N. Abrams, Inc.

Finally, we would like to thank these members of our families particularly: Sarah and Judd Fermi, Gair Fraser, David Aukland, Hy and Victoria Samra, and Mary, Paul, and Kate Davis.

INDEX